BEST OF CLASSIC CARD GAMES

BEST OF CLASSIC CARD GAMES

A Rule and Play Reference for Your Favorite Games

Ash Ryan and C. S. Kaiser

ROCKRIDGE
PRESS

Interior and Cover Designer: Mando Daniel
Art Producer: Megan Baggott
Editor: Van Van Cleave
Production Editor: Jax Berman
Production Manager: Jose Olivera

Author photos courtesy of Dawn Janssen

Paperback ISBN: 978-1-63878-652-8 | eBook ISBN: 978-1-63878-792-1
R0

To my family, for the games
they've taught me.
CSK

For Beanie and Buggie, my
precious gems.
AR

CONTENTS

INTRODUCTION

In a log cabin with no running water or heat, a young boy picked up a deck of cards for the first time. The challenge was clear: win at least one game against a set of formidable opponents (his relatives). The prize? A batch of his great-uncle's world-famous caramel popcorn.

Motivated by such a tasty reward, he would probably have been willing to learn a new language, let alone a new game. And he did win that popcorn. It was some of the best he'd ever had (though he's come to suspect that its "world-famous" status might have been exaggerated). But that's not why the time he spent in an off-the-grid cabin in the middle of the Canadian wilderness became such a landmark moment for him. That day, he discovered not only a lifelong hobby but a passion that would change his life.

For that young boy, day-to-day interactions were a struggle thanks to undiagnosed autism. Trying to act "normal" in the most basic social situations was stressful and nightmarish. Card games became a bridge between the confusing world of human interactions and the structured environment his mind craved. They allowed him to socialize within a system of rules he understood. They helped him sharpen and focus his overstimulated mind—skills that benefit him in many areas of life to this day.

As he got older, he started carrying a deck of cards everywhere he went. It was his way of connecting and breaking the ice with new people. When he was 14, he used it to strike up a game of President with a group of unfamiliar kids at summer camp. One of the boys who joined him for that game became a close friend. Over the next couple of decades, they would spend thousands of hours bonding over games of all types.

Later on, they became the authors of this book.

Not everyone has as dramatic a history with card games as C. S. Kaiser (the boy in the cabin). For most people, card games are a side hobby; a social catalyst; a boredom-crushing activity hidden away when the boss walks by at work. That was the case for Ash Ryan (the friend from camp), though he, too, would claim that card games changed his life. His university years were full of afternoon Cribbage matches and late-night marathons of Hand and Foot Canasta. Those games helped facilitate deep friendships with some incredible people who would one day introduce him to the love of his life—his future wife.

Why tell these stories in the introduction to a book of card game rules? Besides introducing ourselves, we wanted to illustrate some of the benefits that card games can have. We believe they can be a healthy and life-enriching part of any recreational diet. Playing cards can help keep elderly minds sharp. It can teach children important life skills—logic, critical thinking, patience, and emotional self-control, to name a few. Card games help people of all ages practice math, pattern recognition, concentration, and memory skills. Not to mention that they fulfill our human need to play—which, according to neuroscientist Dr. Jaak Panksepp, is not socially engineered but something that is rooted in our DNA (*Affective Neuroscience: The Foundations of Human and Animal Emotions* by Jaak Panksepp, 2004).

Welcome to *Best of Classic Card Games*! We've compiled rules and strategies for 81 of the greatest card games played worldwide. We couldn't include every game that exists, of course, so we selected a broad sample from eight major categories. Some of our favorites include President (fantastic for breaking the ice with groups); Rook and Hearts (strategic games of the trick-taking variety); Klondike, Spider, and Pyramid (perfect solo games for a rainy afternoon, especially when accompanied by an audiobook and some hot tea); childhood favorites War, Cheat, and Slapjack (our younger siblings particularly loved that last one); and Canasta (great for long evenings with close friends). Whether you're looking to brush up on an old favorite or find something completely new, you're bound to find it here.

Card games have a near-magical ability to create friendships and memories that last a lifetime. We hope this book helps you do just that.

Sincerely,

C. S. Kaiser & Ash Ryan

GETTING READY TO PLAY

Because this book is intended for players of all experience levels, including beginners, we'd better lay some groundwork before getting to the actual games. The rules pages will assume the reader knows certain things about card playing, including the basic structure of a game and the meanings of certain terms. All of the prerequisite info can be found here, in the pages that precede chapter 1. We'll conclude by summarizing the categories of games you'll find in the following chapters.

Ready? Let's get started!

CARD GAMES 101

This section covers the essentials you'll need to know in order to play any of the games in this book. We'll explain the features of cards, how they fit together to form combinations, and the structure of a typical game.

The Deck

Every game in this book can be played with standard 52-card decks. These can be purchased from online and retail stores and are typically labeled "playing cards." Prices vary depending on the brand, quality, and design, but an average deck is usually not too expensive. Most of our games require only one deck. When multiple decks are needed, it's best if they're all of the same make, size, and design. There are exceptions, however; some games specifically call for different players to use decks with different backs.

A standard playing card deck has 52 unique cards that are divided into four groups called suits. Each suit contains 13 cards of different ranks. The ranks are the same across all suits, meaning each rank occurs four times. Most decks also contain a few extra cards, including two Jokers. These typically have pictures of clowns or court jesters and are only used in some games.

The side of a card that displays its suit and rank is called the "face." The opposite side, which usually has some sort of colorful design, is called the "back." The backs of all cards in a deck look exactly the same.

Suit is indicated by a graphic symbol (*not* the number or letter) on each card. In a standard deck, the suits are Hearts, Diamonds, Spades, and Clubs. Besides appearance, there is no difference between the suits unless a game's rules specify that they should be treated differently.

Color is related to suit—Hearts and Diamonds are red; Spades and Clubs are black. Though color is not nearly as important as suit or rank, some games have rules regarding card color. (Note that Jokers don't have suit but do have color.)

Rank (sometimes called "face value") is indicated by the number or letter on each card. Unlike suits, ranks *always* have different values and a set order; however, the importance of rank order varies from game to game. Unless the rules say otherwise, Ace (A) is the lowest-ranking card, followed by the number cards (sometimes called "numerals" or "spot cards") in ascending order, Two through Ten. Next come the face cards (or "court cards"), which contain pictures of royalty. In ascending order, the face cards are Jack (J), Queen (Q), and King (K).

The rank order described in the previous paragraph is called "natural ranking." This is a default from which many games deviate. "Aces high," for example, is an extremely common variant in which Ace ranks higher than King instead of below Two.

Numerical values or **point values** are assigned to cards in some games. Although these values are usually attached to rank, the numerical value of a number card isn't always the same as its rank.

Common Card Combinations

Card games often involve grouping cards together in various ways. Here are some common combination types to look out for:

- **SET:** Multiple cards (typically three or four) of the same rank. Sets of five or more are possible when using multiple decks. Subsets of this category include:

    Two of a kind, **pair**, or **set of two**: Two cards of the same rank.

    Three of a kind, **pair royale**, or **set of three**: Three cards of the same rank.

    Four of a kind or **set of four**: Four cards of the same rank.

- **FLUSH:** Multiple cards of the same suit.

- **RUN, STRAIGHT, OR SEQUENCE:** Three or more cards of consecutive rank (for example: Nine, Ten, and Jack). Some games require these cards to all be of the same suit.

- **STRAIGHT FLUSH OR SUIT SEQUENCE:** A run that is also a flush (consecutive card ranks of the same suit).

A Typical Game

Card games have standard practices that all players should be aware of. Bear in mind that these guidelines are not set in stone; they may be overridden by the rules of an individual game. Always read the rules carefully.

Player Arrangement: Players typically sit in a circle at equal distances from one another. If there are two players, they sit opposite each other. The common space between all players is called the "table"; this is where cards are played, shuffled, dealt, discarded, etc. All players should be able to reach the center of the table.

Play Direction: Certain game events move from one player to the next around the table. The direction in which these events move (clockwise or counterclockwise) is called the "play direction." Customary play direction varies depending on where in the world the players live. The player next to the dealer in play direction (to the left or right, depending on whether play progresses clockwise or counterclockwise) is traditionally called the "eldest hand"; however, we will call this player the "starting player," because (unless otherwise specified) they will receive the first card in a deal and take the first turn in a hand.

Games and Hands: A game is composed of one or more hands. The word "hand" actually has two meanings in the context of card games:

1. Cards held by an individual player and kept secret from other players.

2. A portion of a game that takes place between two deals, or between the final deal and the end of the game.

If this ever gets confusing, remember that the two definitions are closely linked: a player usually receives a new hand (definition 1) every hand (definition 2), although the dealer may distribute additional cards within a hand (definition 2). Normally, a player is allowed to pick up and see the values of the cards in their hand (definition 1). In some cases, hands are kept facedown on the table or used in some other way.

Turns: During each hand, players take one or more turns. A turn is a player's chance to perform actions permitted or required by a game's rules. Beginning with the starting player, each player takes their turn one at a time, progressing around the table until the hand is over. In some cases, a player who is unable or unwilling to play may pass, or forfeit, their turn.

Dealing: At the beginning of each hand, a player called the dealer distributes cards to all players. Beginning with the starting player, the dealer places one card facedown in front of each player, moving in a loop around the table and dealing the final card to themselves. This process is repeated until everyone has the correct number of cards. The dealer may have other responsibilities as well, such as arranging cards on the table or distributing additional cards during a hand.

Dealer Rotation: The first dealer is chosen by a random process, such as turning up a card for each player and selecting the person who got the highest card. For each hand that follows, the dealing job shifts to the next player in play direction.

Shuffling: Cards must be shuffled (arranged in a random order) before being dealt or used in a game. This is usually done by the dealer prior to dealing. A simple shuffling method for children and beginners is to spread the cards facedown on the table, mix them around, and randomly gather them back into one pile. A more advanced method called "riffling" starts with splitting the deck roughly in half and holding one portion in each hand. With the backs of the cards toward your palms, grip the shorter ends of the piles with your thumbs and middle fingers. Hold the piles facedown near the surface of the table, brace the backs against your index fingers, and gently pull upward with your thumbs so that the ends gripped by your thumbs curve upward. Finally, with your hands held so that your thumbs are almost touching, roll or slide your thumbs upward along the adjacent edges so that the cards are gradually released. If this is done correctly, the cards of one pile should intermix with those of the other as they snap flat against the table. When the riffle is finished, square the cards into a single, shuffled deck. Repeat this a few times (seven riffles provides optimal randomness). For a clearer demonstration of riffling, we've provided a video tutorial at www.ash-and-kaiser-books.com/how-to-shuffle.

BE THE BEST: HANDLE CARDS LIKE A PRO

Handling cards takes practice. Here are some pro tips for dealing and hand management:

Dealing: Hold the deck facedown in the palm of one hand, gripping the longer sides and pressing your thumb against the top. Using your other thumb, slide the top card away from you and grasp it with your thumb and forefinger. (If it doesn't move, loosen your grip on the deck. If multiple cards push loose, tighten your grip.) Gently slide or toss the card to the appropriate player, taking care to ensure it stays facedown.

Managing Your Hand: Holding your cards close and facing toward you in a fanned pile, pinch the bottom halves between a thumb and forefinger with just enough pressure to keep them together. Sort them in a manner that allows you to quickly access the cards you need. There's no "right way" to do this, but it's common to arrange them by suit, by rank, or in combinations that are relevant to the game being played.

LEARN THE LINGO

If you've read this far, you can already see that cardplaying involves a lot of jargon. Here are some additional terms:

Cut: To split a deck or pile into two parts.

Discard: To remove cards from play or from one's hand, usually by placing them in a designated "discard pile."

Downcard: A facedown card, especially when adjacent to faceup cards.

Draw: To take cards (usually into one's hand) from the stock or some other pile.

Faceup/Facedown: Indicates the direction of the face when a card is laid flat. Also applies to piles.

Fanned: Cards held or piled in a staggered fashion, often so that the ranks and suits are visible.

Follow Suit: To play a card that matches the suit of a previously played card.

In Turn: One at a time, during one's own turn.

Led Suit: The suit of the first card played to a trick.

Look *(as in "look at one's hand")*: To see the faces of cards as opposed to just seeing the backs.

Meld: *(noun)* A group of cards that form a meaningful combination. *(verb)* To arrange or play such a combination.

Misdeal: A deal that is unplayable or unfair due to chance or dealer error. All cards are gathered, reshuffled, and redealt.

Pile: Cards laid on top of one another. Also called a "stack."

Play *(as in "play a card")*: To perform a permitted action with a card.

Shed: To remove cards from one's hand by playing or discarding them.

Squared: A pile of cards with cleanly aligned edges.

Stock: An undealt portion of the deck that will be used in the game.

Tableau: A group of cards arranged on the table for use in the game.

Trick: A group of cards that forms on the table as each player in turn plays one card faceup.

Trump Suit: A suit whose cards outrank those of any other suit, regardless of natural ranks. Cards of the trump suit are called "trump cards." Trump cards of higher natural rank will outrank those of lower natural rank, but the lowest trump card outranks all nontrump cards.

Turn Up: To flip a facedown card faceup.

Upcard: A faceup card, especially when adjacent to facedown cards.

Wild: A card that may represent any rank and suit the holder chooses.

BE THE BEST: MASTER THE ETIQUETTE AND AVOID THE MISSTEPS

Like most social activities, cardplaying has established etiquette and faux pas. Follow these guidelines to ensure a pleasant experience all around:

- **Handle cards with care.** Nobody enjoys playing with dirty or damaged cards! Play with clean hands. Avoid curling, bending, or dropping cards.

- **Wait for the deal to finish.** Only pick up your hand once everyone has theirs.

- **Don't look at other players' cards.** If a player is holding their cards where you might see them accidentally, politely warn them.

- **Stay focused.** Keep track of whose turn it is. When it's yours, don't rush—it's appropriate to take a moment to think—but try not to keep others waiting longer than necessary.

- **Put the phone away.** Be present and engaged!

- **A card laid is a card played.** Taking back moves is bad form. (This may be ignored for young children and beginners.)

- **No "table talk."** Communicating hints or information about your hand to a teammate is a form of cheating.

- **Be a gracious loser (and winner).** While there's nothing wrong with good-natured competition, going overboard ruins the experience for others.

TYPES OF CARD GAMES

We've grouped the games in this book into eight categories based on their objectives and styles of play. Granted, our system is not perfect. Some games overlap categories. Others could be in a category of their own. As a result, you may find that we've categorized some games differently than others (or you) would. Following is a brief overview and explanation of the categories we've chosen.

Capturing Games

Capturing games are those in which the objective is to collect cards. These are some of the easiest games to learn and understand. As such, they are popular among children. Well-known examples include Go Fish, War, Slapjack, and Concentration.

Shedding Games

In a shedding game, the goal is to lose (shed) all of the cards from one's hand, by either discarding or playing them according to the game's rules. Popular examples include President, Crazy Eights, and Uno.

Matching Games

These games involve the collection of specific matches such as sets or runs. In some games, such as James Bond, the game is won by collecting the required matches. In others, such as Cribbage, Canasta, and Rummy, points are awarded for collecting matches and the winner is determined by overall score.

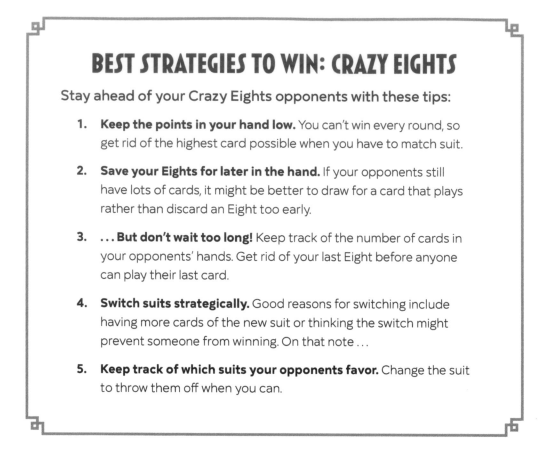

BEST STRATEGIES TO WIN: CRAZY EIGHTS

Stay ahead of your Crazy Eights opponents with these tips:

1. **Keep the points in your hand low.** You can't win every round, so get rid of the highest card possible when you have to match suit.

2. **Save your Eights for later in the hand.** If your opponents still have lots of cards, it might be better to draw for a card that plays rather than discard an Eight too early.

3. **...But don't wait too long!** Keep track of the number of cards in your opponents' hands. Get rid of your last Eight before anyone can play their last card.

4. **Switch suits strategically.** Good reasons for switching include having more cards of the new suit or thinking the switch might prevent someone from winning. On that note...

5. **Keep track of which suits your opponents favor.** Change the suit to throw them off when you can.

Patience Games

Klondike. FreeCell. Spider. Tri Peaks. If you've ever been bored in front of a computer, you probably recognize some of these names. Patience, or solitaire, games are one-player card games in which the objective is to "solve" a particular arrangement of cards rather than overcome an opponent. (There's some luck involved; for most of these games, not every arrangement is solvable.) Our chapter for this category will include many single-player classics as well as a few multiplayer variants.

BEST STRATEGIES TO WIN: KLONDIKE SOLITAIRE

Besides being a fun way to pass the time, Klondike is an exercise in mental endurance and critical thinking. Here are five tips for success:

1. **Draw immediately.** This has zero risk and could increase your available moves.

2. **Only make meaningful moves.** Not every possible move is a good move. Some might even hinder you. Only perform moves that increase your possibilities or result in meaningful progress, such as uncovering tableau cards or freeing up a desired card in the draw pile.

3. **Freeing up tableau cards is priority one.** When given a choice of cards to turn up, choose the one that sits on a larger column of downturned cards.

4. **Avoid moving useful cards to foundation piles.** If there are red Sevens in play, don't remove a black Eight that could be used for building down.

5. **Wait for a King before emptying a column.** Empty spaces gain you nothing if there are no Kings to fill them.

Trick-Taking Games

You've probably seen card tricks before, but we're not talking about magic here. A trick-taking game is one in which each player, one at a time, selects a card from their hand and plays it faceup on the table. This forms a group of cards called a "trick." Playing the first card to a trick is called "leading" the trick. The suit of the first card played to a trick, called the "led suit," is important in many games. When everyone has played to the trick, the winning card of the trick is determined according to the game's rules. Whoever played the winning card "takes" the trick, placing it into a pile with any other tricks they've taken. This is often the player that leads the next trick. Typically, all players have the same number of cards at the start of a hand, and the hand ends when they play their last cards to form a final trick. Popular games of this type include Hearts, Spades, Euchre, Bridge, and—a personal favorite of ours—Rook.

Vying Games

Casinos. Poker tournaments on late-night television. Smoky back rooms in gangster movies. These are a few places one might expect to see vying games being played. Of course, they can also be played "just for fun" at a kitchen table. The objective of a vying game is to win chips from your opponents by having—or convincing them that you have— a better hand than they have. As you may have guessed, this category includes many versions of poker, including Five-Card Stud, Follow the Queen, and Texas Hold'em.

Banking Games

Banking games, which include popular casino games like Blackjack and Baccarat, are by far the most luck-based of all the games in this book. In this type of game, a single player called the "banker" (who is also the dealer) plays one-on-one against every other player in the game. Each nonbanking player's objective is to win chips from the banker by placing bets on certain aspects of the game, such as whether or not their hand will beat the dealer's. Bets are declared by placing betting chips in designated spots on the table. When a player wins a bet, the banker pays them one or more times the amount they bet. When they lose a bet, the banker takes the chips the player placed on the table. In some situations, a player may keep their bet chips without gaining additional chips.

BEST STRATEGIES TO WIN: POKER

Poker is as much about personality and psychology as it is about cards and chips. Playing "just for fun" isn't necessarily good practice; people play differently when they know nothing's at stake. Here are some basic strategies for when you're ready to start playing to win:

1. **Learn the odds.** Be prepared for as many scenarios as possible. Knowing your chances is the key to playing strong.

2. **When in doubt, fold.** Don't waste chips wagering on an unlikely win.

3. **Bluff on and off.** Don't be predictable. Control what the other players think they know about you. (Psychology, remember?)

4. **Play aggressively when your opponent falters.** Their weakness is your opportunity.

5. **Don't play at all if you're not focused.** *You'll* be the one showing weakness.

   And here's a bonus tip for playing in tournaments:

6. **Don't spend your early hands playing defensively.** In order to progress, you need to build up a stack of chips. To do that, you need wins!

When banking games are played in casinos, everything is preset and the banker is a casino employee. When playing at home, distribute chips to all players and establish minimum and maximum bet amounts. To ensure a fair game, each player should assume the banker role for a set number of hands.

Fishing Games

Fishing games involve playing cards from one's hand against a tableau of faceup cards on the table. By creating matches, players can capture cards from the table. Because fishing games tend to enjoy strong regional popularity, we suspect there will be many in this book that you've never heard of. Perhaps you'll be the first to introduce your friends to Seep, Laugh and Lie Down, Chinese Ten, or Eléwénjewé!

BE THE BEST: HOSTING GAME NIGHT

Card games are a great excuse to get people together. Without the right planning, though, your fun night could become a disaster. Here are some tips for hosting a fantastic game night:

Pick games ahead of time. Not knowing what game you're playing delays the fun. You want to make sure your guests will enjoy themselves. Find out what games they like beforehand and plan things out before they arrive.

Invite lots of people. Large games can be a lot of fun, and you can always get multiple games going if needed. Just make sure you have enough chairs and play spaces!

Prepare for groups of different sizes. If people leave early or want to sit out after a while, you don't want to wind up shorthanded.

Choose the right snacks. Nothing sticky, powdery, or otherwise likely to get all over the cards or the table.

Keep the rules handy. This saves time if there's a disagreement. Actually, there's a book we could recommend . . .

HOW TO USE THIS BOOK

Each following chapter will feature 9 to 11 games from one of the categories just described. Within each chapter, games are sorted by difficulty level from easiest to hardest.

Every rules page has the same general structure. Look for the following bullet points and headings:

Bidding: Specific instructions on bidding (not to be confused with betting).

Difficulty: A classification of *easy, medium,* or *hard* based on factors like rule complexity and the amount of strategy required.

Number of Players: How many players the game is designed for. Limitations can sometimes be overcome by adding more decks or modifying rules; options may be listed under "Variations."

Length of Play: A rough estimate of how long it takes to play a hand or whole game.

Materials: The required number of decks and anything else needed.

Card Ranking: Information about relative card ranks. If natural ranks are used, we will specify "Aces high" or "Aces low." If the ranks are not natural, we will list them in descending order or provide a detailed explanation.

Numerical Card Values: Any numerical values that are attached to specific cards.

Betting Type: Indicates whether a vying game uses fixed-limit or spread-limit betting (see Poker Basics, page 156).

Objective: The end goal of the game.

Setup: Any preparation that is required before the first hand begins.

The Showdown: For vying games, this section will contain rules relating to the final stage of a hand, in which player cards are revealed and a winner is determined.

Dealing: Directions for the dealer each time a hand is dealt. (For some games, this will be incorporated into "Playing the Game.")

Playing the Game: A detailed breakdown of the rules and procedures of the game.

Tableau Layout: Instructions on how to arrange cards on the table in patience games.

Variation(s): Alternative versions or common house rules.

That's it for laying the groundwork. Now feel free to flip to the chapter that most interests you, or just turn the page and start at chapter 1. You could be moments away from discovering your new favorite game!

CHAPTER 1

CAPTURING
GAMES

BEGGAR MY NEIGHBOR

2 TO 6 PLAYERS   **EASY** | **LENGTH OF PLAY:** TYPICALLY, UNDER 15 MINUTES

(CAN GO MUCH LONGER)

This is a simple, luck-based game great for waiting rooms or road trips with children.

OBJECTIVE: Capture every card in the deck.

MATERIALS: One standard 52-card deck (no Jokers); with 4+ players, add another deck

Dealing

Deal the whole deck into facedown piles, one in front of each player. (Some piles may be one card short.) Players may square their piles but must not look at or rearrange the cards.

Playing the Game

In turn, each player turns up the top card from their pile onto a central pile. If a player turns up a face card or Ace, the next player must pay a "penalty" by turning up a certain number of cards:

1. Jack: 1 card

2. Queen: 2 cards

3. King: 3 cards

4. Ace: 4 cards

If, while paying a penalty, a player turns up another face card or Ace, their penalty stops. The next player must now pay a penalty based on the last turned-up card. If a player does not turn up a face card or Ace while paying a penalty, the player who made them pay the penalty wins the central pile, adding it to the bottom of their own pile.

When a player's pile is empty, they are out of the game. Last player standing wins!

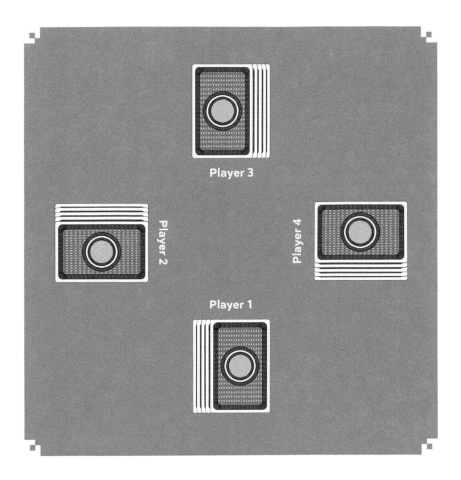

CONCENTRATION

Concentration is a fantastic game for young children and can also be played solo as a simple yet effective memory exercise.

OBJECTIVE: Find every matching pair on the table.

MATERIALS: One standard 52-card deck (Jokers optional)

Dealing

Deal the entire deck facedown on the table. (This requires about six square feet of free space if the cards are spaced half an inch apart. Most tables or floor spaces should accommodate this.) Typically, the cards are arranged in a grid, but almost any organized layout will work. A standard deck without Jokers will fill a grid of 4 cards by 13 cards. If Jokers are included, a grid of 6 by 9 can be used. Other dimensions can be used if you don't mind having incomplete rows or columns.

Playing the Game

When playing with two or more players, each player turns up two table cards, one after the other, on their turn. If the cards are the same rank and color, the player captures them into a scoring pile in front of them and takes another turn. Otherwise, the cards are turned facedown and the next player takes their turn. When all table cards are captured, count the collected matches to determine a winner, or (especially when playing with little ones) just celebrate the fact that you beat the game together.

When playing solo, a single player takes a series of turns until the table is cleared. For an added challenge, try to clear the table in the fewest turns or least amount of time possible.

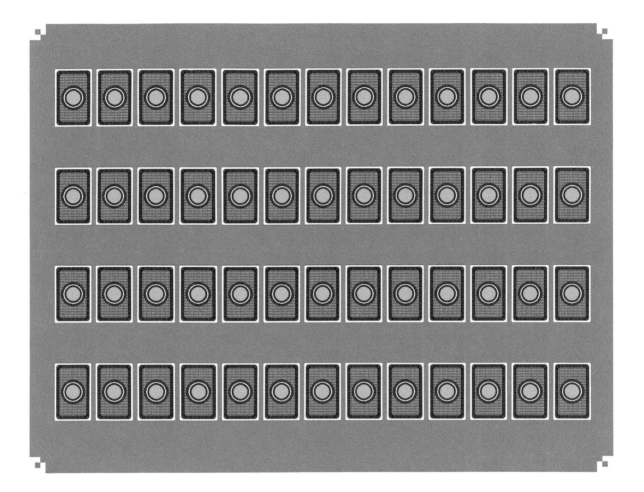

GO FISH

This simple classic is often the first card game kids learn.

OBJECTIVE: Collect the most pairs.

MATERIALS: One standard 52-card deck (Jokers optional)

Dealing

With up to three players, deal seven cards to each player's hand. With four or more players, deal five cards to each. Spread the remaining cards facedown on the table, forming a "pond."

Playing the Game

Each player begins their turn by asking another player whether they have a card of a specific rank (for example, "Sam, do you have a Three?"). The asking player must have a card of that rank in their hand. If the asked player has the requested card in their hand, they give it to the player who asked. Otherwise, they reply, "Go fish!" and the asking player "fishes" (draws) a card from the pond. In either case, the current player's turn ends.

When a player obtains a pair (whether by drawing, asking, or receiving it from the deal), they place it beside them in a scoring pile. If a player's hand becomes empty for any reason, they draw five cards from the pond on their next turn. When all cards have been matched into pairs, the player with the most pairs wins.

Variation

A common household rule grants players another turn if drawing or requesting a card yields a pair.

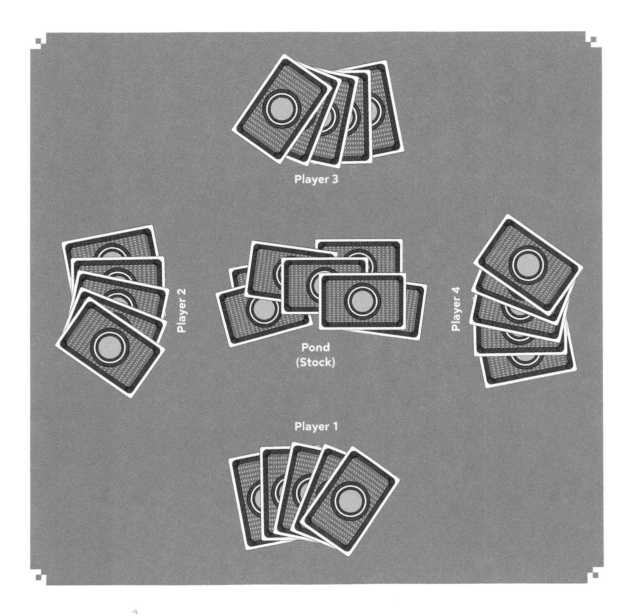

Player 3

Player 2

Pond
(Stock)

Player 4

Player 1

MY SHIP SAILS

Offering a slight step up from Go Fish (page 24) in terms of complexity, My Ship Sails is a great choice for introducing children to suit matching and basic cardplaying strategy.

OBJECTIVE: Be the first to collect seven cards of the same suit.

MATERIALS: One standard 52-card deck (no Jokers)

CARD RANKING: Natural, Aces high

Dealing

Deal seven cards to each player's hand. The dealer keeps the stock.

Playing the Game

A hand consists of a series of turns during which all players play at the same time. Each turn has two steps:

1. First, each player chooses a card from their hand and discards it, facedown, within easy reach of the next player.

2. After all players have discarded, each player *except for the dealer* picks up the card that was discarded by the previous player and adds it to their hand. The dealer draws a new card from the stock.

Because the dealer doesn't draw the previous player's discards, these cards will accumulate in a pile. If the stock becomes empty during a hand, the dealer shuffles this discard pile and forms it into a new stock. At the end of a turn, any player who has seven cards of the same suit may declare "My Ship Sails" and reveal their hand. If they are the only one to do so, they win. If multiple players say "My Ship Sails" after the same turn, the game is won by the player who holds the highest-ranking card.

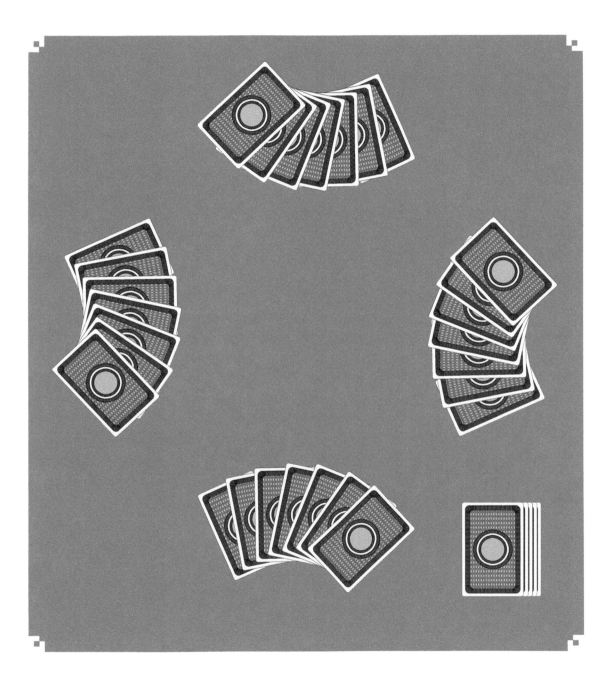

SLAPJACK

2+ PLAYERS   **EASY** | **LENGTH OF PLAY:** 10 TO 15 MINUTES

Slap Jacks, get cards. Maybe don't use your favorite deck for this one.

OBJECTIVE: Capture every card in the deck.

MATERIALS: One standard 52-card deck (Jokers optional)

Dealing

Deal the whole deck into facedown piles, one in front of each player. (Some piles may be one card short.) Players may square their piles but must not look at or rearrange the cards.

Playing the Game

Each player in turn draws the top card from their pile and adds it, faceup, to a central pile. Players must draw away from themselves so they don't see the card's value before everyone else. If the drawn card is a Jack, every player tries to be the first to slap the central pile with the hand *not* used to draw cards. Whoever slaps the central pile first takes the whole thing, shuffles it, and adds it to the bottom of their own pile.

If a player slaps on a card that is not a Jack, they must give a card from their pile to the player who played the slapped card. If a card is played on top of a Jack before anyone has a chance to slap, the Jack is lost (it's too late to slap). When a player runs out of cards, they have one chance to get back in the game by winning the next slap. If a Jack turns up and they fail to slap first, they are out. Last player standing wins.

Variations

- **Snap:** Please see page 30.

- **Harsher Penalty:** When a player slaps on a card that is not a Jack, the central pile is divided evenly among all other players.

- **Shout & Slap:** Players must shout "Slapjack" while slapping the pile or their slap is invalid.

WAR

2 PLAYERS   **EASY** | **LENGTH OF PLAY:** 10+ MINUTES (CAN GO VERY LONG)

Rapid and luck-based, this is a great one for beginners.

OBJECTIVE: Capture every card in the deck.

MATERIALS: One standard 52-card deck (Jokers optional)

CARD RANKING: Natural, Aces high (if included, Jokers outrank Aces)

Dealing

Deal the whole deck into two facedown piles, one for each player. Players may square their piles but must not look at or rearrange the cards.

Playing the Game

Turns are taken simultaneously. Each turn, both players turn up the top cards from their piles and play them onto the table. Whoever played the higher-ranking card wins both cards and adds them to the bottom of their pile, ending the turn. However, if both cards are the same rank, a "war" is declared. Both players play three cards facedown and one faceup. Whoever played the higher-ranking of the most recently turned-up cards wins the war, capturing all cards played during the turn (including the original pair). If the new upcards are also a pair, the war carries on (both players play three more downcards and one upcard). This continues until somebody wins the war and ends the turn.

Play continues until one player captures all of the cards. If a player runs out of cards during a war, they lose the war (and also the game, because they have no more cards).

SNAP

2+ PLAYERS   **EASY** | **LENGTH OF PLAY:** 10 TO 15 MINUTES

Nobody wearing a gauntlet containing six gems of power may play this game.

OBJECTIVE: Capture every card in the deck.

MATERIALS: One standard 52-card deck (Jokers optional)

Dealing

Deal the whole deck into facedown piles, one in front of each player. (Some piles may be one card short.) Players may square their piles but must not look at or rearrange the cards.

Playing the Game

Each player in turn draws the top card from their facedown pile and places it faceup in an adjacent pile. When a pair is visible on top of any two piles, the first player to shout "Snap" wins both piles. These are added to the bottom of their facedown pile.

If multiple players shout "Snap" at the same time, place one of the matching piles on top of the other and place the combined pile in the center of the table. If another card turns up that is a match for this pile, the first player to shout "Snap pool" wins the central pile plus the matching pile.

When a player's facedown pile is empty, they have one chance to successfully shout "Snap" to get back in the game. If a pair turns up and they fail to claim it first, they are out of the game. Last player standing wins.

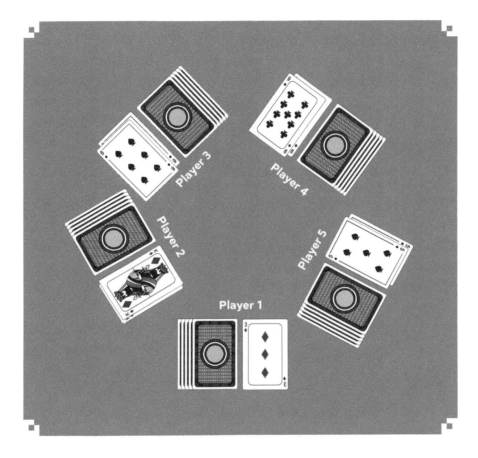

EGYPTIAN RAT SCREW

2 TO 6 PLAYERS | **MEDIUM** | **LENGTH OF PLAY:** 10+ MINUTES

Also called Slap, this game is essentially Beggar My Neighbor with some Slapjack rules added to make it more interesting and fun.

OBJECTIVE: Capture every card in the deck.

MATERIALS: One standard 52-card deck (no Jokers); with 4+ players, add another deck

Dealing

Deal the whole deck into facedown piles, one in front of each player. (Some piles may be one card short.) Players may square their piles but must not look at or rearrange the cards.

Playing the Game

This game is played exactly like Beggar My Neighbor (page 20) but with a Slapjack-like twist: Players may capture the central pile by slapping it when consecutive cards form certain combinations. A valid slap overrides a player winning the pile because they played a face card or Ace.

The following Slapjack rules apply:

♦ Players must draw *away* from themselves.

♦ Slapping is done with the hand *not* used to draw cards.

♦ If a combo that could be slapped is covered by another card, it's too late to slap.

♦ When a player runs out of cards, they have *one* chance to get back in the game by winning a slap. If they fail to slap first or their next slap is invalid, they are out of the game.

If a player realizes they've slapped when they shouldn't have, they must add one card from their pile to the bottom of the central pile. If a player believes their slap is valid and wishes to take the central pile, other players can challenge the slap and examine the last few played cards. If the slap turns out to be valid, each challenger gives one card to the player who slapped. If not, the player pays a card to each challenger and does not receive the pile.

The difficulty of the game can be adjusted by increasing or decreasing the number of valid card combinations. Before the game begins, players must agree on which combinations to use. The following are commonly used (feel free to invent your own if you like):

- Double: A pair.

- Sandwich: A pair with a third card in between.

- Hoagie: A pair with two other cards in between.

- Pair of Royals: Any two face cards stacked one on top of the other.

- Top Bottom: A card whose rank is the same as the bottom card of the pile.

- Tens: Two cards whose ranks add up to 10, with Ace counting as one. (Optional: One or more face cards may be played between the two numbers.)

- Run: Establish beforehand how many cards these must contain and whether they may be ascending, descending, or both.

- Flush: Establish beforehand how many cards these must contain.

- A Joker (if included)

Variation

A common variation requires players to touch their slapping hand to their forehead before slapping. This may be instituted for all players or only those who are caught making invalid slaps.

GOPS (GAME OF PURE STRATEGY)

Also known as Goofspiel (a German word that literally translates to "goof game") or Psychological Jujitsu, GOPS is easy to learn but involves more strategy (and far less luck) than most capturing games.

OBJECTIVE: Score the most points by collecting "prize cards."

MATERIALS: One standard 52-card deck (no Jokers); with 4+ players, add another deck

CARD RANKING: Natural, Aces low

Setup

Split the deck(s) into piles, each containing one full suit.

Dealing

Choose one suit pile to be the "prize" pile. Shuffle it and place it facedown in the center of the table. Each player takes one of the other suit piles as their hand. (These do not need to be shuffled.) Any remaining suit piles are not used.

Playing the Game

The game is played in 13 turns (one for each prize card). Each turn, the top card on the prize pile is turned up. Players bid on the upturned prize card by selecting a card from their hand and holding it facedown in front of them. When every player has selected their bid, all bid cards are turned up at the same time. Whoever played the highest-ranking bid card wins the prize card and places it in a scoring pile in front of them. The played bid cards are discarded, and a new turn begins.

If multiple players are tied for the highest bid, the current prize card is placed beside the prize pile and carried forward to the next turn. The winner of the next bid wins all of the active prize cards (the one for the current turn plus any that were carried forward from previous turns). If a tie occurs in the final turn of the hand, nobody wins the active prize cards; they are discarded.

After 13 turns, the players add up the point values of their prize cards:

- **13 points** per King

- **12 points** per Queen

- **11 points** per Jack

- **1 point** per Ace

- **Points equal to the rank value** of each number card

The player whose scoring pile is worth the most wins.

Variations

- **Aces High:** Ace counts as 14 points instead of 1.

- **No Prize Pool:** Instead of carrying them forward to the next turn, prize cards are discarded in the case of a tie.

- **No Ties Allowed:** When a tie for highest bid occurs, the tied bids are ignored, and the next-highest bid wins the prize. If all bids are tied, discard or carry forward the prize card.

- **Target Score:** Play multiple hands with cumulative scoring. The winner is the first to reach a preset target score.

- **SWOPS** (Switch on Paired Spots)**:** A variation for two players in which the players swap hands when their bids are tied.

- **Bid:** A two-player variation that incorporates the following rule changes:

  - The prize pile contains two suits instead of one. (The game is still played in 13 turns, so much of the prize pile remains unused.)

  - Aces are worth 15 points rather than 1.

  - When bids are tied, the bid cards are discarded and the players rebid for the same card. (A new prize card is not added.)

CONTINUED

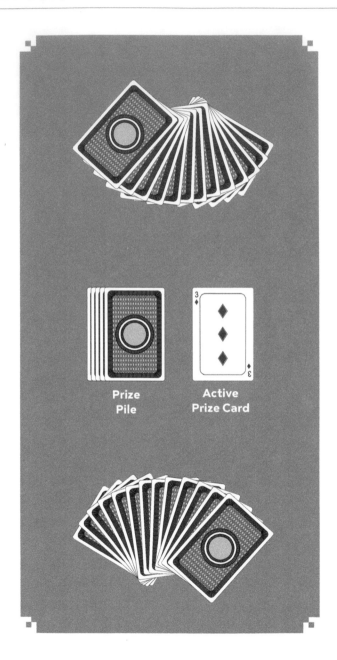

Prize
Pile

Active
Prize Card

SIX-CARD GOLF

2+ PLAYERS   **MEDIUM** | **LENGTH OF PLAY:** 5 TO 15 MINUTES PER HAND

Many people wonder why this game is called "golf." Apparently, it's because you play nine "holes" and try to get the lowest score. (Using golf clubs is not recommended, although a cart may be helpful for retrieving snacks.)

OBJECTIVE: Have the lowest score after nine hands.

MATERIALS: One standard 52-card deck with Jokers, a scorekeeping method; with 4+ players, add another deck

Dealing

Deal six cards to each player's hand. Players do not pick up or look at their hands. Place the stock facedown in the middle of the table and turn up the top card beside it to start a faceup discard pile.

Playing the Game

At the start of a hand, each player arranges their cards in a grid of two rows by three columns. Then, they turn up any two of their six cards. On each turn, they do one of the following:

- ◆ Take the top card from the discard pile and swap it for a card in their hand.

- ◆ Draw the top card from the stock and swap it for a card in their hand.

- ◆ Draw the top card from the stock and discard it.

The player may look at a drawn card before deciding what to do with it. They may *not* look at a facedown card in their hand before replacing it. However, if they choose to discard the drawn card, they may (but are not required to) turn up one of their downcards.

Cards swapped into a hand are always played faceup, regardless of what they replace. Cards swapped out of a hand are placed faceup on the discard pile. When one player's hand is fully turned up, every other player gets one more turn. Then, the hand ends and all players turn up all of their cards. Any two cards of the same rank in the same column (including Jokers) are worth zero points. Otherwise, players receive points for their cards as follows:

CONTINUED

- **0 points** per King

- **10 points** per Jack or Queen

- **Points equal to the rank value** of each number card

- **1 point** per Ace

- **−2 points** per Joker

Each player's score for the hand is added to their total score for the game. The player with the fewest points after nine hands wins.

Variations

- **Back Nine:** Play 18 hands for a longer game.

- **No Jokers:** Without Jokers, the Two is worth −2 points instead of 2.

- **Double Eagle:** Four of a kind in a hand is worth −10 points, or adds 10 points to everyone else's score.

- **Four-Card Golf:** Players have four cards in a 2x2 grid and turn up two of them after a deal. When a player is ready for the hand to end, they knock on the table (this takes up an entire turn). Every other player gets one more turn.

- **Eight-Card Golf:** Players have eight cards in a 4x2 grid. Otherwise, this version is the same as Six-Card Golf.

- **Nine-Card Golf:** Players have nine cards in a 3x3 grid and turn up three of them after a deal. Pairs in a column no longer count as zero points; instead, three of a kind in a single column must be present. Optionally, these may also count on rows or diagonals.

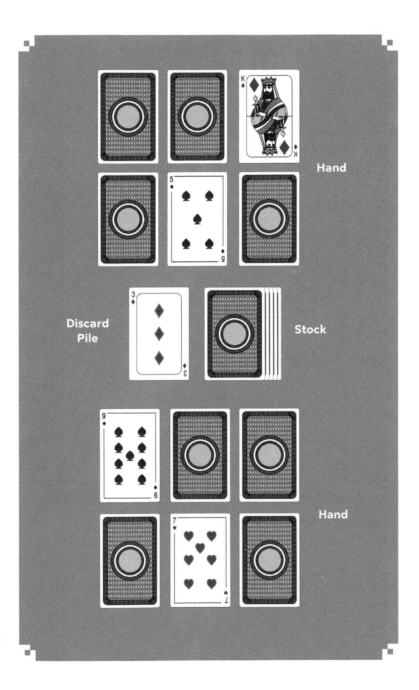

Hand

Discard
Pile

Stock

Hand

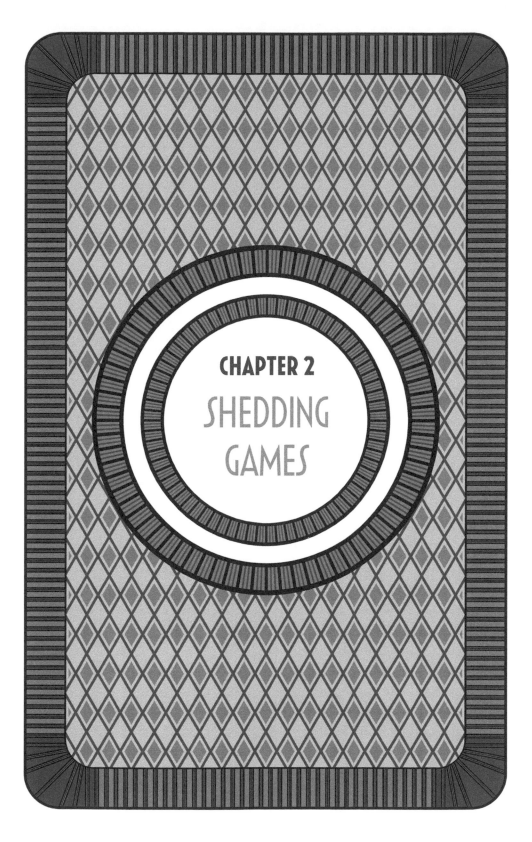

CHAPTER 2

SHEDDING
GAMES

CHEAT

3 TO 10 PLAYERS   **EASY** | **LENGTH OF PLAY:** 5 TO 10 MINUTES

Also known as I Doubt It or Bluff, this one is fun because you're *supposed* to cheat.

OBJECTIVE: Be the first to run out of cards.

MATERIALS: One standard 52-card deck (no Jokers); with 6+ players, add another deck

CARD RANKING: Natural, Aces low

Dealing

Deal the entire deck into hands for all players. (Some hands may be one card short.)

Playing the Game

In turn, each player discards one or more cards in a central, facedown discard pile. Starting with Aces, the card rank that must be discarded increases by one each turn. After the 13th turn, in which a player must discard Kings, the required rank loops back to Aces.

As they are discarding, each player declares the rank and number of cards. Players may bluff and discard more or different cards than what they state aloud. Passing turns is not permitted; if a player doesn't have their required discard, they *must* bluff.

If a player suspects another of bluffing, they may call "cheat" before the next player plays. The top discards are checked. If the accused player *was* bluffing, they must take the entire discard pile into their hand. Otherwise, the accuser must take the discard pile. The first player to empty their hand wins. (Watch out, though; getting a "cheat" call on your final discard is almost guaranteed.)

CATCH THE THIEF (OLD MAID)

2+ PLAYERS   **EASY** | **LENGTH OF PLAY:** 5 TO 10 MINUTES

The Joker has been stolen! Don't get caught with it . . .

OBJECTIVE: Don't get stuck holding the Joker.

MATERIALS: One standard 52-card deck with one Joker

Dealing

Deal the whole deck into hands for all players. (Some hands may be one card short.)

Playing the Game

After the deal, all players immediately discard any pairs in their hands. On their turn, each player chooses a card at random from the hand of the previous player, who should hold their hand within reach of the choosing player without allowing them to see the faces of the cards. The choosing player adds the selected card to their hand. If it creates a pair, the pair is discarded. If they still have cards in their hand, they hold their hand out for the next player to choose a card.

When a player's hand is empty, they are out of the game; they take no further cards and are safe from losing. If the previous player's hand is empty, a player takes a card from the most recent player who still has cards. When all pairs have been matched and discarded, one player will be left holding the Joker. This player is the "thief" who stole the valuable Joker card; they lose the game! (For fun, you could say a player has been "framed" if they accidentally took the Joker from another player. They still lose, though.)

Variations

- **Color Match:** Pairs may only be discarded if the card colors match.

- **Donkey's Rear:** Instead of including a Joker in the deck, remove the Jack of Diamonds. Color match rules apply. Whoever holds the Jack of Hearts at the end loses.

- **Monkey-Monkey:** Like the previous variant except a random card is removed so nobody knows which card is unmatched. Color match rules are optional.

GO BOOM

This shedding game is also a simple trick-taking game. If you're new to trick-taking games, please see the brief overview on page 11.

OBJECTIVE: Be the first player to reach 100 points.

MATERIALS: One standard 52-card deck (no Jokers), a scorekeeping method

CARD RANKING: Natural, Aces high

Dealing

Deal seven cards to each player's hand. Place the stock facedown in the center of the table.

Playing the Game

The starting player leads the first trick. In turn, every other player must play a card that matches the lead card's suit or rank. If they don't have one, they must draw cards from the stock until they can play. If the stock is empty, a player who can't play passes their turn. Whoever played the highest-ranking card of the lead card's suit takes the trick and plays the lead card for the next trick.

When a player plays their last card, they announce it by saying "Boom!" The hand ends immediately. The player who "boomed" earns points for all cards remaining in other players' hands:

- ◆ **10 points** per face card

- ◆ **1 point** per Ace

- ◆ **Points equal to the rank value** of each number card

A player's score for a hand is added to their total score for the game. The first player to reach 100 total points wins.

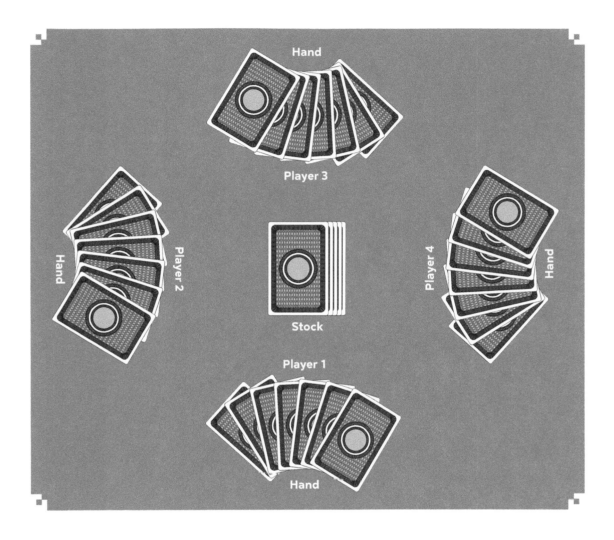

Hand

Player 3

Hand

Player 2

Stock

Player 4

Hand

Player 1

Hand

SEVENS

This Domino-type game comes to a very satisfying conclusion if all players are allowed to finish.

OBJECTIVE: Be the first to run out of cards.

MATERIALS: One standard 52-card deck (no Jokers)

CARD RANKING: Natural, Aces low

Dealing

Deal the entire deck into hands for all players. (Some hands may be one card short.)

Playing the Game

Players achieve the objective by building 13-card suit sequences—rows of cards running from Ace to King, all of one suit—on the table. The player holding the Seven of Diamonds starts the game by playing it onto the table. The next player may build onto the Diamonds sequence by placing the Six or Eight on either side of the Seven, or they may play the Seven of a different suit to start a new sequence. Play continues in this manner, with each player in turn building one card onto an existing sequence or starting a new sequence. A player must play on their turn if they are able; if they have no cards that they can play, they pass.

The first player to run out of cards is the winner. If desired, the remaining players may continue until everyone is out of cards.

Variation

- **Around the Corner:** Aces are both high and low and sequences may extend beyond them.

The Deal

Played Cards

PRESIDENT

Also called Janitor, Scum, Putz, and other (often less savory) names, President is the perfect party game thanks to its simple rules and lively game play.

OBJECTIVE: Be the President for as long as possible.

MATERIALS: One standard 52-card deck, Jokers included; with 9+ players (or if you feel like flooding the game with cards), add one or more additional decks

CARD RANKING: Joker, Two, Ace, King down to Three

Setup

If playing with multiple decks, shuffle them together. Draw cards to determine initial rank placement. Following the play direction, players arrange themselves by rank in descending order. The top rank is President and the lowest is Scum. When you have five players or more, the second-highest rank becomes Vice President and second-lowest is Vice Scum. All other players are Citizens.

Dealing

Scum shuffles and deals the entire deck into hands for all players. *If anyone touches their cards before the deal is complete, they automatically become Scum in the next hand.*

Playing the Game

After the deal, Scum must give the President the two *best* cards in their hand. (This means giving up their Jokers or whatever their two highest-ranking cards are.) In return, the President gives Scum any two cards they want from their hand. (If playing with a Vice President and Vice Scum, these players swap one card in the same manner.)

Once the swap is done, the President starts a round of turns by laying down a set containing any number of cards of the same rank. (In this case, sets of one are allowed. Sets of more than four are allowed if playing with multiple decks.) In turn, every other player around the table must play a higher-ranking set containing the same number of cards, or pass their turn. Playing a single Joker beats any set and immediately ends the turn. Otherwise, the round ends when everyone has played or passed. The player who played the highest-ranking set (the last player to lay down cards) starts the next round of turns.

The first player to run out of cards becomes President in the next hand. The rest of the players continue to play and receive increasingly lower ranks as they run out of cards. The last player holding cards is the next Scum.

Variations

- **Less Powerful Jokers:** This works best with multiple decks. Instead of a single Joker beating any set, Jokers must be played in sets, but a Joker set can contain one fewer card. (No, you can't claim you're playing "zero Jokers" to beat a set of one. Believe us; we've tried.)

- **Second Term:** Instead of stopping a round when everyone has taken one turn, anyone who hasn't passed may play again in normal turn order. This continues until all but one player has passed.

- **Change the Scoring:** To make things more competitive, assign a number to each seat around the table, with the President's seat having the highest value and Scum's having the lowest (either 0 or –1). At the end of each hand, each player receives points equal to their *new* seat value.

CONTINUED

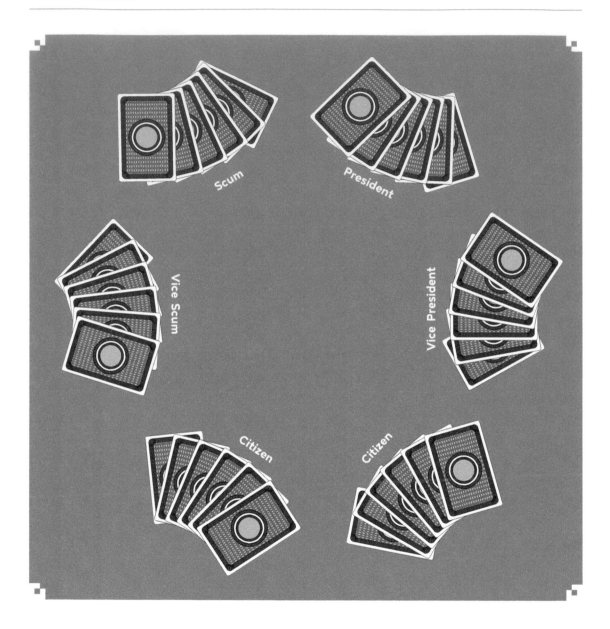

ROLLING STONE

Also known by its French name Enflé, which means "swollen" or "inflated," this simple shedding and trick-taking game has been described as both "maddening" and "one of the best children's games." If you're new to trick-taking games, please see the brief overview on page 11.

OBJECTIVE: Be the first to run out of cards.

MATERIALS: One standard 52-card deck (no Jokers)

CARD RANKING: Natural, Aces high

Setup

The required number of cards depends on the number of players:

+ With **four players**, remove the Twos, Threes, Fours, Fives, and Sixes from the deck.

+ With **five players**, remove the Twos, Threes, and Fours.

+ With **six players**, only remove the Twos.

Dealing

Deal eight cards to each player's hand.

Playing the Game

The starting player leads the first trick. All other players must follow suit in turn. Whoever played the highest card of the led suit takes the trick, discards it, and leads the next trick. If a player is unable to follow suit, they collect the cards already played to the current trick, add them to their hand, and start a new trick. The first player to play their last card is the winner.

Variation

+ **Keeping Score:** Play multiple hands with the winner of each earning points for the cards remaining in their opponents' hands (1 for Aces, 10 for face cards, rank value for number cards).

CRAZY EIGHTS

2+ PLAYERS   **MEDIUM** | **LENGTH OF PLAY:** 10 TO 30 MINUTES

They're not actually crazy. They just have eccentric taste in suits.

OBJECTIVE: Have the lowest score when another player reaches 100 points.

MATERIALS: One standard 52-card deck (no Jokers), a scorekeeping method; with 4+ players, add another deck

Dealing

If there are only two players, deal seven cards to each player's hand. If there are three or more players, deal five cards to each. Place the stock facedown in the middle of the table and turn up the top card beside it to start a faceup discard pile. If the upcard is an Eight, shuffle it back into the stock and turn up a new card.

Playing the Game

In turn, each player discards (plays) a card from their hand that matches the previous discard's rank or suit. If they can't discard, or choose not to, they must draw cards one at a time from the stock until they make a discard or the stock is empty. When the stock is empty, a player who can't or won't discard passes their turn.

Eights (the "crazy" cards) may be discarded on top of any card. These cards are "suit wild"; in other words, they may represent any suit the player of the Eight wishes. The player must declare a suit when playing an Eight, and the next player must discard a card of that suit.

When any player runs out of cards, the hand is over. The other players receive points based on the cards still in their hands:

- **50 points** per Eight

- **10 points** per face card

- **1 point** per Ace

- **Points equal to the rank value** of each number card

Each player's score for the hand is added to their total score for the game. When any player reaches a total score of 100 or more, the player with the lowest score wins.

Variations

♦ **Uno** (page 61) is a game based on Crazy Eights that includes fun action cards and special rules.

♦ **Hollywood Eights:** This game uses an alternate scoring method in which the goal is to be the first to reach 100 points. Unplayed cards are not worth any points; instead, points are awarded for each card a player discards:

   ♦ 20 points per Eight

   ♦ 15 points per Ace

   ♦ 10 points per face card

   ♦ Points equal to the rank value of each number card

CONTINUED

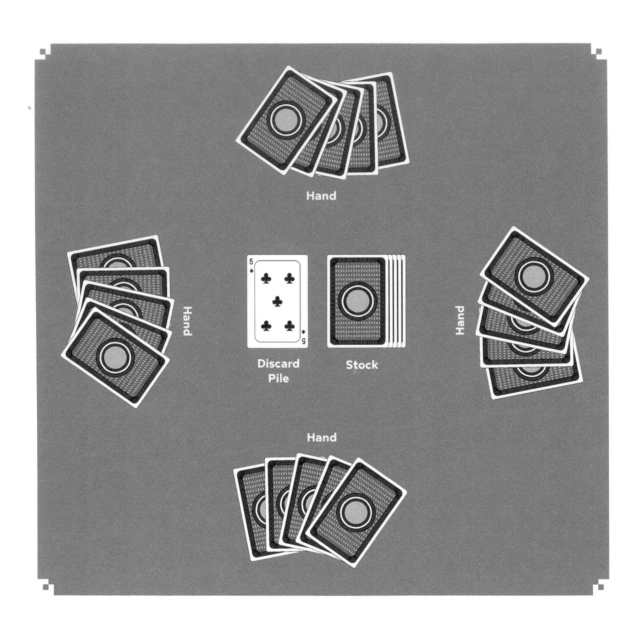

MICHIGAN

3+ PLAYERS   **MEDIUM** | **LENGTH OF PLAY:** 5 TO 10 MINUTES PER HAND

This game has a rich history, having evolved from a 19th-century game called Newmarket, which developed from an 18th-century game called Pope Joan.

OBJECTIVE: Win more chips than the other players.

MATERIALS: Two standard 52-card decks (no Jokers), betting chips

CARD RANKING: Natural, Aces high

Setup

Distribute an equal number of betting chips to each player. The exact number doesn't matter, but bear in mind that each player will spend a *minimum* of four chips per hand. We recommend 20+ for each player.

From one deck, take the Ace of Hearts, King of Clubs, Queen of Diamonds, and Jack of Spades. Place them in the center of the table, faceup. These are called "boodles"; they will remain where they are throughout the entire game. Place the remainder of this deck aside (it will not be used).

Dealing

Deal the entire second deck into hands for all players, plus one extra hand next to the dealer (the "widow hand"), which should be dealt to first. (Some hands may be a card short.)

Playing the Game

At the start of a hand, the dealer places two chips on each boodle. All other players place one chip on each boodle. After dealing, the dealer has the option to swap their hand for the widow hand. If the dealer passes on the widow hand, the other players may bid for it. Players bid one at a time in turn order. They may bid an amount of chips or pass, but passing doesn't prevent them from bidding in the future, when the bid returns to them. Bidding continues around the table until nobody is willing to bid higher than the most recent bid. The highest bidder pays the chips they bid to the dealer and swaps their hand for the widow hand.

CONTINUED

The starting player selects from their hand a card that is the lowest they have of any one suit. The card may be of any rank as long as they don't have a lower one of the same suit. (They may have lower cards of a different suit.) This card is played faceup on the table in front of them.

Whoever has the next card of the same suit (one rank higher than the played card) plays it in the same manner. This repeats until the Ace is played or nobody has the next card. This is called a *stop*.

When a stop occurs, the last player to play a card starts a new sequence in the manner explained above. The new sequence must be of a different suit than the sequence that just ended. If the player is unable to play a card of a different suit, play passes to the next player who is able to.

When someone plays a card that is identical to one of the boodles, they win the chips on that boodle. When any player plays their last card, they win the hand. Every other player pays the winner one chip for each card left in their hand. Any chips remaining on the boodles are carried forward into the next hand.

Play for a set number of hands or until all but two players are out of chips. Whoever has the most chips at the end wins!

Player 3

Player 4

A
♥

K
♣

Q
♦

J
♠

Boodles

Player 2

Player 5

Player 1

Widow
Hand

SPIT

A game of speed, awareness, dexterity, and (thankfully) no actual spitting.

OBJECTIVE: Be the first to run out of cards.

MATERIALS: One standard 52-card deck (no Jokers)

Dealing

Give half the deck (26 cards) to each player.

Using these cards, each player deals themselves a row of five stock piles. Each player's leftmost pile contains one card; the next contains two cards; and so on until the fifth pile, which contains five cards. The top (or only) card in each stock pile is turned faceup while the rest are facedown.

Each player's undealt cards become their spit cards. These can be placed in a facedown pile or held in one hand. Players must not look at any of their cards except the five turned up on the stock piles. The "spit cards" held by the player (not to be confused with the "spit piles" in the middle) are only played to start the spit piles, or to restart game play when both players have run out of legal moves (i.e., neither one can move a card from a stock pile to a spit pile).

Playing the Game

There are no turns in this game; both players play whenever they can, as fast as they can.

When a player is ready to start, they say the word "spit." When both players have said it, they turn up their top spit cards at the same time. These are placed beside each other in the middle of the table, forming the start of two spit piles. Both of these should be equally distant from both players.

Players may only use one hand to play their cards and may only move one card at a time. A card from the stock piles may be played on a spit pile if it is one rank above or below the top card of that pile. Aces are both high and low; in other words, they can be played on both Twos and Kings, and vice versa. Cards may not be removed from the spit piles once played.

Players can play onto either spit pile as they are able, but if both players try to play on the same spit pile at the same time, the first card to touch the pile is considered played. The other must be returned to where it started.

When a player removes the top card from one of their stock piles, they must turn up the card beneath. If a stock pile is empty, the top card from another stock pile may be moved to the empty space. If neither player can make a valid move, they say "spit" again. When both have done so, whoever has spit cards remaining turns up their next one onto the spit pile they started and play resumes as normal.

A hand ends when a player empties all five of their stock piles, or when both players run out of spit cards and neither can make a valid move. When one of these conditions is met, each player claims one of the spit piles by slapping it. If both players go for the same pile, the player whose hand is underneath wins the pile; the other player takes the unclaimed pile. (Hint: You want to claim the smaller pile!)

Then, both players shuffle their claimed pile together with any stock and spit cards they have left. From this new pile, they deal themselves five new stock piles. Any undealt cards become their spit cards for the next hand.

If a player starts a hand with 15 cards or fewer, they will not be able to start a spit pile and may have an incomplete set of stock piles. In this case, deal as much of the stock pile row as possible, starting with the smaller piles and moving to the larger.

When there's only one spit pile and a player empties their stock piles, no slapping happens; the spit pile automatically goes to the other player. If the player who started with no spit cards is the one who emptied their stock piles, they are completely out of cards and have won the game.

CONTINUED

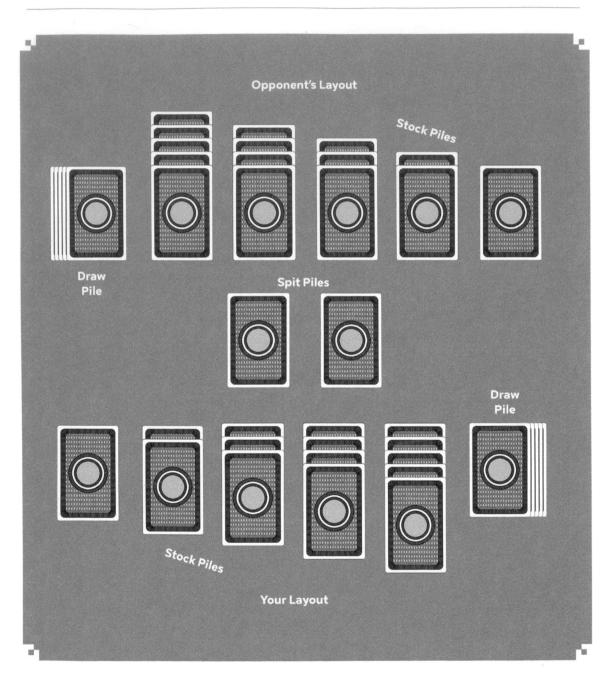

Opponent's Layout

Stock Piles

Draw
Pile

Spit Piles

Draw
Pile

Stock Piles

Your Layout

UNO

Though similar in many ways to Crazy Eights, Uno has action cards and special rules that make for an extra fun time.

OBJECTIVE: Be the first player to reach 500 points.

MATERIALS: Two standard 52-card decks (no Jokers), a scorekeeping method

Setup

Shuffle the two decks together.

Dealing

Deal seven cards to each player's hand. Place the stock facedown in the middle of the table and turn up the top card beside it to start a faceup discard pile.

Playing the Game

In turn, each player discards (plays) a card from their hand that matches the previous discard's suit and/or rank. If they can't discard, or choose not to, they draw one card from the stock into their hand. If the drawn card plays, they may play it. Either way, their turn is over.

Certain cards cause special effects when played or turned up as the first discard:

- **Ten:** Skips the next player's turn.

- **Jack:** Reverses the play direction from clockwise to counterclockwise or vice versa. (In a two-player game, this has no effect on turns. Therefore, some players choose to treat the Jack like a Ten when there are only two players.)

- **Queen:** The next player must draw two cards and may not discard.

- **King:** May be discarded on top of any card and represent any suit the holder wishes. The player must declare a suit when a King is played; the next player must discard a card of that suit. If a King is turned up as the first discard, the first player chooses the suit.

CONTINUED

♦ **Ace:** May be played like a King and has the same suit-changing effect. In addition, it forces the next player to draw four cards and lose their chance to discard. If it is turned up as the first discard, shuffle it back into the stock and turn up a new card.

An Ace may only be played if the holder has no other cards that play. When an Ace is played, the next player may challenge the play. If challenged, the player who played the Ace privately shows their hand to the challenger. If the play was legal, the challenger draws six cards instead of four. If the play was not legal, the player of the Ace draws four cards and the challenger takes a normal turn.

When a player has only one card left, they must say "Uno!" loudly enough for all players to hear. If they don't and are caught before the next player starts their turn, they must draw two cards as a penalty. The hand ends when any player plays their last card. The player with the empty hand earns points for the cards remaining in other players' hands as follows:

♦ **50 points** per King or Ace

♦ **20 points** per Ten, Jack, or Queen

♦ **Points equal to the rank value** of each number card

A player's score for a hand is added to their total score for the game. The first player to reach a total score of 500 points wins.

Variation

♦ **Mad Jokers:** One or more Jokers (worth 40 points each) may be added to the deck and given their own effects. Possibilities include:

  ♦ **Limited Wild:** The Joker can be played on any card but doesn't change the suit.

  ♦ **Hand Swap:** The player of the Joker may swap hands with any opponent.

  ♦ **Wild Shuffle:** All hands are collected, shuffled together, and redistributed evenly among the players. The player of the Joker chooses the active suit.

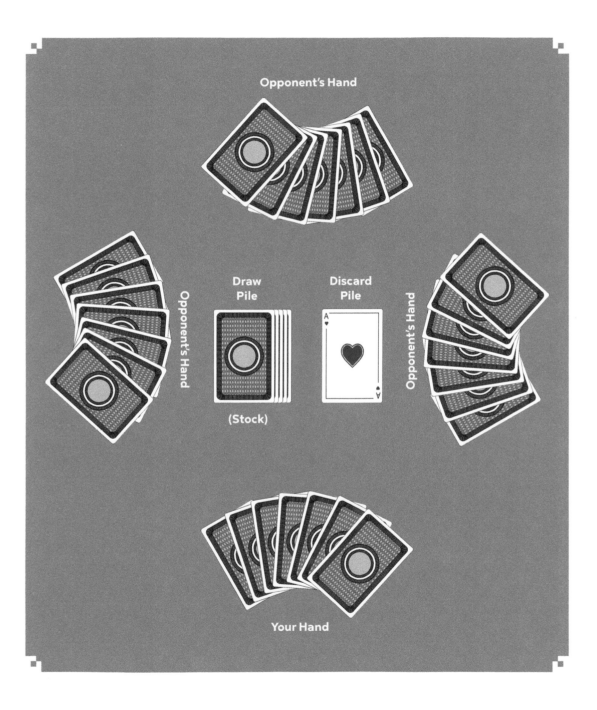

Opponent's Hand

Opponent's Hand

Draw
Pile

Discard
Pile

A
♥

A

(Stock)

Opponent's Hand

Your Hand

SPEED

This quick game is great for "best of three" tournaments.

OBJECTIVE: Be the first to run out of cards.

MATERIALS: One standard 52-card deck (no Jokers)

Dealing

Deal a 5-card hand and a 15-card draw pile to each player. In the middle of the table, equally distant from both players, deal four facedown piles in a row. The first and fourth (the "outer piles") should have five cards each. The others (the "inner piles") should have one card each.

Playing the Game

There are no turns in this game. After simultaneously turning up the inner piles, both players play cards from their hands onto both inner piles as quickly as possible. A card may be played on an inner pile if it is one rank above or below the top card of that pile. Aces may be played on both Twos and Kings, and vice versa. If neither player can make a valid move, they simultaneously turn up the top cards from the outer piles and move them onto the inner piles. Play then continues as normal.

After playing a card from their hand, a player must replace it with a new one from their draw pile. The first player to deplete their hand after depleting their draw pile wins.

CHAPTER 3

MATCHING
GAMES

CARD BINGO

2+ PLAYERS   **EASY** | **LENGTH OF PLAY:** 2 TO 10 MINUTES

It's like Bingo, only without the stamps, balls, and other bulky equipment. All you need are two decks of cards!

MATERIALS: Two standard 52-card decks (no Jokers)

Setup

Both decks are shuffled separately. One player is designated the "caller." This player may choose to participate fully in the game or just perform the caller duties.

Dealing

From one deck, the caller deals five faceup cards to each player. (If desired, and if the number of players allows it, the number of cards dealt can be increased for a longer game.)

Playing the Game

From the second deck (not the one used to deal), the caller draws one card at a time and calls out the suit and rank. If any player has a card of the same suit and rank, they turn it facedown. The first player to turn down all of their cards calls "Bingo!" and wins the game.

Variations

- **13-Card Bingo:** Players are arranged in groups of four. Each group is given a deck from which each player is dealt 13 cards. The caller also has a deck. According to Pagat.com, the Doncaster Whist Club in England once played this game with around 60 people!

- **No Suits:** Only ranks are called. Players turn down all cards of the called rank. (Simultaneous wins are possible.)

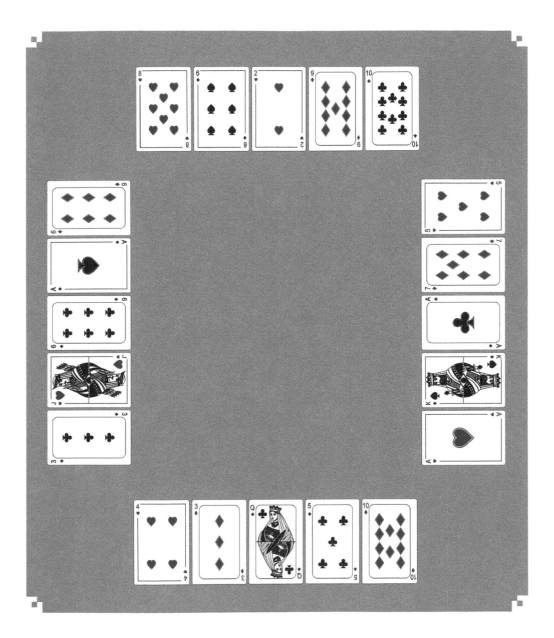

JAMES BOND

Some call it Atlantis. Some call it Chanhassen. We call it Bond. James Bond.

OBJECTIVE: Be the first player to collect a full set of four-of-a-kind matches.

MATERIALS: One standard 52-card deck (no Jokers)

Dealing

Deal four cards faceup in the center of the table. Deal the rest of the deck into facedown piles containing four cards each. Distribute the piles evenly to all players. (Alternately, distribute the rest of the deck evenly between the players. Players will then deal their own four-card piles facedown.) Players keep their piles in a row in front of them.

Playing the Game

There are no turns in this game; all players play at the same time. When the dealer says "go," each player picks up one of their facedown piles like a hand. One at a time, they may trade cards from their hand for faceup cards on the table, first laying the card from their hand faceup and then picking up the table card. At any time, they may place their current pile facedown, pick up another of their facedown piles, and trade cards from it in the same manner. Piles may never exceed four cards, and players may not hold more than one pile at once. The first player to collect four of a kind in every pile and shout "James Bond" wins. Piles are turned up at the end to prove the win is legitimate.

Player 2

Player 1

SPOONS

This one is a fantastic party game in the tradition of games like Donkey and Pig. (Come to think of it, those names cogently sum up the kind of experience you're in for!)

OBJECTIVE: Don't get eliminated.

MATERIALS: One standard 52-card deck (no Jokers), spoons numbering one fewer than the number of players

Health & Safety Notice

In our experience, this game can get a little crazy. Tug-of-wars may result as players fight over that last spoon. Try not to let things get too rough! Establish some ground rules beforehand so that nobody winds up going to the hospital. If in doubt, remember that plastic spoons are safer than metal ones!

Setup

Pile the spoons in the center of the table.

Dealing

Deal four cards to each player's hand. The dealer keeps the stock.

Playing the Game

The dealer draws the top card from the stock and either swaps it for a card in their hand or discards it. The discard is placed facedown between the dealer and the next player. The dealer immediately draws another card. Meanwhile, the next player picks up the card that the dealer discarded, decides whether to swap it into their own hand, and discards a card beside them for the next player. This pattern continues around the table until the discard reaches the last player before the dealer, who discards into a facedown discard pile next to the stock.

At this point, all players should be playing (drawing, swapping, or discarding) at the same time. Depending on how fast everyone plays, piles may start building up between the players. Regardless, each person may only pick up one card at a time. When the stock is empty, the dealer replaces it with the last player's discard pile and continues drawing.

When a player has four of a kind in their hand, they take a spoon from the center. They may do this as stealthily or obviously as they like. After the player with four of a kind has taken a spoon, all others try to take a spoon as quickly as possible. (Touching a spoon is not sufficient; the player must be the undisputed holder of the spoon for it to count.) If the first player to take a spoon does so in error (perhaps they panicked or got faked out by a gesture from another player), they lose the hand. Otherwise, the player who doesn't get a spoon loses the hand and receives one letter in the word "spoon." A player is out once they've received all five letters (remove a spoon when this happens). Last player standing wins!

Variations

- **Extreme Spoons:** Place the spoons in some weird location, such as under the table or in another room. (We are not responsible for missing limbs.)

- **Wild Jokers:** Add in Jokers as wild cards.

KEMPS

A clandestine spy mission in card game form!

OBJECTIVE: Be the first team to score five points.

MATERIALS: One standard 52-card deck (no Jokers)

Setup

Players pair up in teams of two. Teammates sit opposite each other. Each team secretly agrees on a nonverbal signal to indicate, "I have four of a kind."

Dealing

Deal four cards to each player's hand. Place the stock facedown. Turn up the top four cards and arrange them in a 2×2 grid in the middle of the table.

Playing the Game

Everyone plays at the same time, swapping one card at a time between their hand and the table. When it's clear nobody wants the current table cards, the dealer discards them and turns up four new ones.

If a player believes their partner has four of a kind, they call "Kemps!" If the partner does have four of a kind, their team gains a point. If not, they lose a point. If a player believes a different team has four of a kind, they call "cut!" If any of their opponents has four of a kind, the team of the player who called "cut" wins a point. Otherwise, they lose a point.

Between hands, teams may change their signals if they wish. The first team to score five points wins.

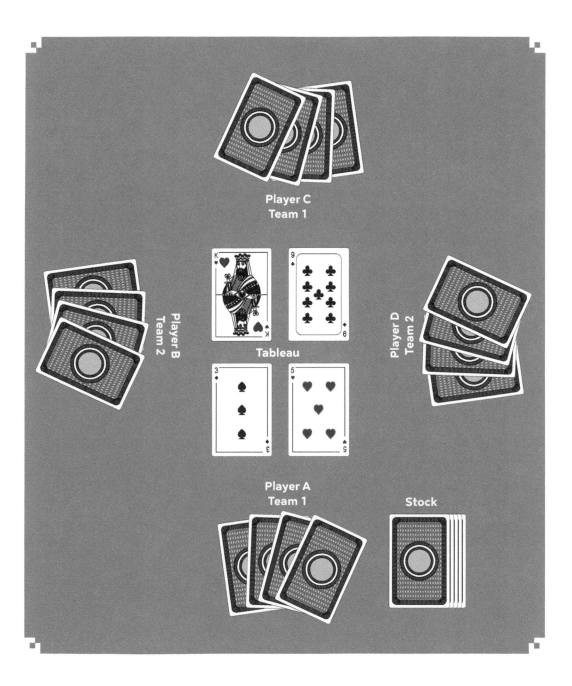

Player C
Team 1

Player B
Team 2

Tableau

Player D
Team 2

Player A
Team 1

Stock

RUMMY

Rummy has so many variations that it's become an entire genre, with multiple subfamilies of games. Gin Rummy, one of the most popular spin-offs, can be found on page 79.

OBJECTIVE: Be the first player to reach 100 points.

MATERIALS: One standard 52-card deck (no Jokers), a scorekeeping method

CARD RANKING: Natural, Aces low

Dealing

Deal a hand for each player according to the following table:

Number of Players:	2	3	4	5	6
Size of Hand:	10 cards	7 cards	7 cards	6 cards	6 cards

Place the stock facedown in the middle of the table and turn up the top card beside it to start a faceup discard pile.

Playing the Game

A player's turn consists of four steps:

1. **Drawing:** The player takes the top card from either the stock or the discard pile.

2. **Melding:** The player may play "melds" from their hand onto the table. A meld is a set or run containing three cards or more. All cards in a run must be of the same suit. Each meld is laid faceup in a fanned pile.

3. **Laying Off:** The player may add eligible cards from their hand to existing melds on the table, including those laid down by opponents. Sets can be built out in either direction (ascending or descending).

4. **Discarding:** The player discards a card from their hand faceup on the discard pile. This signals the end of the player's turn. If they drew from the discard pile, they may not discard the same card they drew.

Melding and laying off are always optional; a player may hold on to cards that play in the hope of gaining bonus points for playing all of their cards at once later on. (This is a riskier strategy, however; they'll pay a big penalty if they're stuck holding a lot of cards at the end of the hand.)

If the stock is empty at the start of a player's turn, they may either draw from the discard pile or refresh the stock by flipping the discard pile facedown. If they choose the latter, they draw the top card of the new stock and start a new discard pile with their end-of-turn discard.

Play continues until one player empties their hand, or "goes out," which ends the hand. Discarding is optional on the turn a player goes out. When a player goes out, they receive points based on the cards still in their opponents' hands:

♦ **10 points** per face card

♦ **1 point** per Ace

♦ **Points equal to the rank value** of each number card

If a player goes out without melding or laying off any cards, it's called "going rummy," and the number of points the player earns for the hand is doubled. A player's score for a hand is added to their total score for the game. The first player to reach 100 or more total points wins.

Variations

To add more variety to basic Rummy, try one or more of these common rule variations:

♦ **Meld First:** Players may not lay off unless they have played at least one meld in the current hand, either on the current turn or a previous turn. Players achieve "going rummy" by laying off cards on the same turn as their first meld. So, on their final turn, they could (a) meld all of their cards, or (b) meld some cards and then lay off the rest. (Both ways can be done with or without a discard.)

♦ **Limited Melding:** Only one set or run can be melded per turn.

♦ **Mandatory Discard:** Players must discard when going out.

CONTINUED

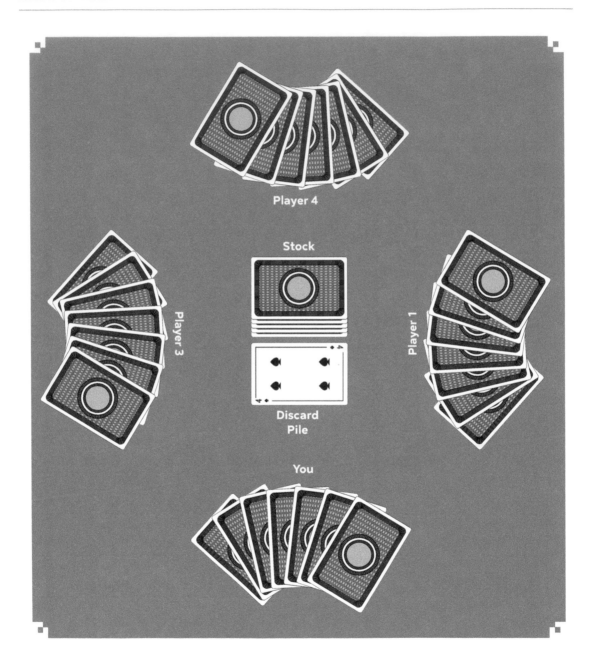

Player 4

Stock

Player 3

Player 1

Discard
Pile

You

GIN RUMMY

This version of Rummy (page 76) is one of the most popular two-player games in the world.

OBJECTIVE: Be the first player to reach 100 points.

MATERIALS: One standard 52-card deck (no Jokers), a scorekeeping method

CARD RANKING: Natural, Aces low

Dealing

Deal 10 cards to each player's hand. Place the stock in the middle of the table and turn up the top card to start a faceup discard pile.

Playing the Game

A player's hand consists of melds and "deadwood" (cards not part of a meld). Their goal for each hand is to create melds and reduce their deadwood. A meld is a set or run containing three cards or more. All cards in a run must be of the same suit. Individual cards may not be used in more than one meld. The deadwood has a total point value based on the cards contained within it:

- **10 points** per face card

- **1 point** per Ace

- **Points equal to the rank value** of each number card

A player's turn consists of drawing one card, either from the stock or the discard pile, and then discarding one card faceup on the discard pile. Before discarding, if their deadwood is worth 10 points or fewer, they may "knock," which ends the hand. (Knocking is optional; a player may choose to keep playing and further reduce their deadwood.) If they choose to knock, the player physically knocks on the table or says "knock." Then, they discard a card (traditionally, facedown) and lay their hand faceup, separating the melds from the deadwood. The opposing player now has the opportunity to "lay off" some of their deadwood cards by building them onto the knocking player's melds.

CONTINUED

When the laying-off is complete, the point values of the deadwood in both hands are scored and compared. If the knocking player's deadwood is worth fewer points, they win points equal to the difference between the two values. If the other player's deadwood is worth fewer points, they have "undercut" the knocker and win a 10-point bonus on top of the difference between the two deadwood values. The player who loses a hand becomes the dealer for the next hand. If neither player knocks before there are only two cards left in the stock, the hand is a draw and the dealing job passes from the dealer to the other player.

A player who knocks may be able to play 10 cards of only melds with no deadwood. This is called "going gin" and awards the player a 25-point bonus plus the value of the other player's deadwood. The opposing player is not allowed to lay off any cards. If a player goes gin with 11 cards (in other words, without discarding after knocking), it's called a "big gin." This is scored the same as a regular gin, but with a 50-point bonus.

A player's score for a hand is added to their total score for the game. The first player to reach 100 or more total points wins.

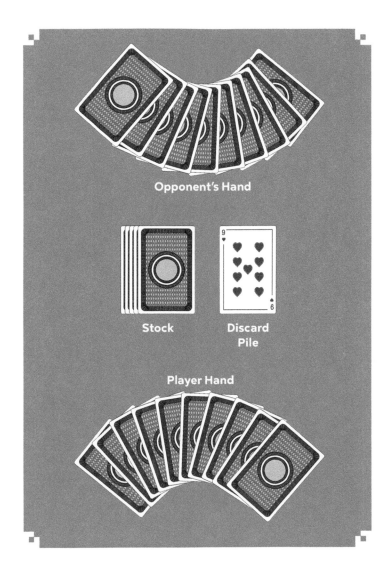

Opponent's Hand

Stock

Discard
Pile

Player Hand

BEZIQUE

2 PLAYERS   **HARD** | **LENGTH OF PLAY:** 5 TO 10 MINUTES PER HAND

A direct ancestor of Pinochle (page 85), Bezique belongs to the trick-and-meld family of games. If you're new to trick-taking games, please see the brief overview on page 11.

OBJECTIVE: Be the first player to reach 1,000 points.

MATERIALS: Two standard 52-card decks (no Jokers), a scorekeeping method

CARD RANKING: Ace, Ten, King down to Seven; with trump suit

Setup

Remove all Sixes, Fives, Fours, Threes, and Twos from both decks. Shuffle the remainder together.

Dealing

Deal eight cards to each player's hand by giving each a batch of three, a batch of two, and another batch of three. Place the stock facedown, turn up the top card, and slide it partway beneath the remaining stock. This card's suit is the trump suit for the hand.

Playing the Game

A hand is played in two phases, both of which consist of a series of tricks. In the first phase, the non-dealer leads the first trick, and the second person to play on any trick has no obligation to follow suit or play trump cards. If no trump cards are played on a trick, whoever played the higher-ranking card of the led suit wins the trick. Otherwise, the player of the higher-ranking trump card wins it. If both cards are identical, whoever led the current trick wins it. The winner of a trick takes both cards into a facedown scoring pile. Then, they may (optionally) declare and play one of the following melds. If they play a meld, they immediately add the appropriate number of points to their total score:

Melds		
Declaration (Meld Type)	Cards Melded	Points Scored
"Trump Seven"	Seven of the trump suit (may be swapped for the faceup card beneath the stock if the player wishes)	10
"Marriage"	King and Queen of a nontrump suit	20
"Royal Marriage"	King and Queen of the trump suit	40
"Bezique"	Queen of Spades and Jack of Diamonds	40
"Double Bezique"	Two Beziques	500
"Four Jacks"	Any four Jacks	40
"Four Queens"	Any four Queens	60
"Four Kings"	Any four Kings	80
"Four Aces"	Any four Aces	100
"Sequence"	Ace, Ten, King, Queen, and Jack of the trump suit	250

Melds are placed on the table but still considered to be part of the player's hand. The cards can be played on future tricks and used in future melds. However, an individual card can't be used more than once for the same *type* of meld in the same hand. For example, if a Jack of Diamonds is used in a Bezique, it could later be used in a Four Jacks, Double Bezique, or Sequence, but not another Bezique. (The *other* Jack of Diamonds, however, could be used in a second Bezique with the Queen of Spades that wasn't used in the first Bezique.)

If a meld pushes a player's total to 1,000 points, they immediately win. Otherwise, after the meld (or right after taking the trick, if they didn't meld), the winner of the trick draws the top card from the stock. The other player draws the next card. Finally, the winner of the trick leads the next trick and the entire trick-and-meld process repeats.

CONTINUED

The second phase begins when the winner of a trick draws the final stock card. The other player takes the faceup trump card beneath. Both players pick up their melded cards and play eight more tricks in which the nonleader *must follow suit* if possible. If they *can* follow suit, they *must play a higher-ranking card than the leader* if possible. If they *can't* follow suit, they *must play a trump card* if possible. Players do not play melds after tricks in the second phase. The winner of the final trick scores 10 bonus points. Both players score 10 points for each Ten or Ace they captured in tricks throughout the hand. When one or both players have reached 1,000 total points, the player with the higher score wins.

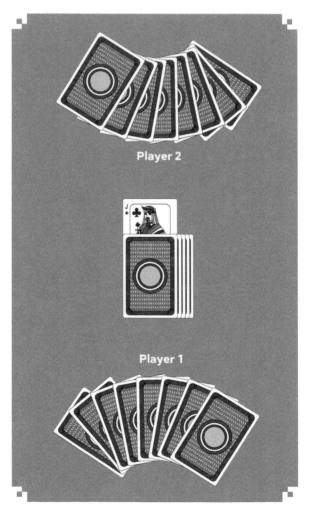

PINOCHLE

4 PLAYERS   **HARD** | **LENGTH OF PLAY:** 10 TO 20 MINUTES PER HAND

Although it's become fairly standard, this is technically a variation called Partnership Auction Pinochle. Classic Pinochle is almost identical to Bezique (page 82). If you're new to trick-taking games, please see the brief overview on page 11.

OBJECTIVE: Be the first team to reach 1,500 points.

MATERIALS: Two standard 52-card decks (no Jokers), a method for recording scores and bids

CARD RANKING: Ace, Ten, King down to Nine; with trump suit

Setup

Remove the Eights, Sevens, Sixes, Fives, Fours, Threes, and Twos from both decks. Shuffle the remaining cards together. Players pair up in teams of two. Teammates sit opposite each other.

Dealing

Deal 12 cards to each player's hand, distributing them in batches of three at a time. A player who is dealt more than four Nines may request a redeal.

Playing the Game

After the deal, players look at their hands and bid to choose the trump suit for the hand. The starting player automatically bids 200. Each player in turn must make a higher bid or pass. Bids must be divisible by 10. Players may not bid after passing. When three players have passed, the bid winner chooses the trump suit. Their team must earn the bid amount in points during the hand or pay a penalty.

When bidding is complete, the partner of the bid winner selects three cards that they believe will help the bid winner meld or take tricks during the hand. These are passed to the bid winner, who then passes any three cards back to their teammate.

CONTINUED

Next, each player finds the highest-scoring melds they can form using the cards in their hand. Starting with the bid winner, each player in turn reveals their melds and records the points earned from them:

Melds			
Category	Type	Cards Melded	Points Scored
Sequence	Common Marriage	King and Queen of a nontrump suit	20
	Royal Marriage	King and Queen of the trump suit	40
	Run	Ace, Ten, King, Queen, and Jack of the trump suit	150
	Double Run	Two Runs	1,500
Set	"Forty Jacks"	Four Jacks of different suits	40
	"Sixty Queens"	Four Queens of different suits	60
	"Eighty Kings"	Four Kings of different suits	80
	"One Hundred Aces"	Four Aces of different suits	100
	"Four Hundred Jacks"	Eight Jacks	400
	"Six Hundred Queens"	Eight Queens	600
	"Eight Hundred Kings"	Eight Kings	800
	"One Thousand Aces"	Eight Aces	1,000
Special	Dix*	Nine of the trump suit	10
	Pinochle	Queen of Spades and Jack of Diamonds	40
	Double Pinochle	Two Pinochles	300

*pronounced "deece"

Multiple melds of the same type are allowed as long as they use different cards. Individual cards may be used in multiple melds across different categories but not within the same category. In other words, a player's cards can be arranged to form sequence melds, then rearranged into set melds, then rearranged once more into special melds.

After the melding comes a trick-taking phase. The bid winner leads the first trick. Everyone else plays to the trick in turn and must follow suit if possible. If they can't, they must play a trump card if they have one. If they don't have a trump card, they may play any other card. Whoever played the highest-ranking card of the led suit takes the trick unless one or more trump cards were played, in which case the highest-ranking trump card wins the trick. If two identical cards are played, the one played first outranks the other. The player who takes a trick leads the next trick of the hand. The team that takes the final trick earns 10 bonus points. Both teams earn 10 points for each Ace, Ten, and King they took in tricks.

Finally, both teams calculate their score for the hand by adding together their melding and trick-taking scores. The team that didn't win the bid adds this amount to their total score for the game. The bid-winning team does the same *if* their score for the hand met or exceeded their bid. If it didn't, they earn *zero* points for the hand and *subtract* their bid amount from their total score for the game. (Negative scores are possible.) The first team to reach a total score of 1,500 points wins. If both teams reach 1,500 points on the same hand, the team that won the bid wins the game.

CANASTA

Canasta is a great choice for those who enjoy longer, more involved games. If you want a bigger version that uses five decks, try Hand and Foot (page 92).

OBJECTIVE: Be the first team to reach 5,000 points.

MATERIALS: Two standard 52-card decks with Jokers, a scorekeeping method

Setup

Shuffle the decks together. Players pair up in teams of two. Teammates sit opposite each other.

Dealing

Deal 11 cards to each player's hand. Place the stock facedown in the middle of the table and turn up the top card beside it to start a faceup discard pile. If the upcard is a Joker, Two, or red Three, turn up another card on top of it. Repeat if necessary.

Card Properties

Rank	Point Value	Special Rules
Joker	50	Wild cards. Can represent any rank in a meld. Discard pile cannot be taken when one of these is on top.
Two	20	
Ace	20	Natural meld cards.
King, Queen, Jack, Ten, Nine, Eight	10	
Seven, Six, Five, Four	5	
Black Three	5	Cannot be melded. Discard pile cannot be taken when one of these is on top.
Red Three	100	Cannot be melded or discarded. Must be played immediately if drawn or received in the deal. When played, a new card is drawn to replace it.

Melds

Melds are sets of three or more cards that may or may not contain wild cards. Each team can play one meld of each rank. Melds with wild cards are called "mixed" or "black"; those without wilds are called "natural" or "red." Wilds may never outnumber the natural cards in a meld. Melds containing fewer than seven cards are laid faceup in a fanned pile. When a seventh card is added, the meld becomes a "canasta" and is squared up to indicate that it is complete. Set the color of the top card to indicate the type of canasta: red for natural, black for mixed. Further cards may be added to canastas as long as they never exceed three wild cards.

Each hand, a team's first meld must contain a minimum number of points. The minimum value of this meld depends on the team's current total score:

Team Score:	Less than 1,500	1,500 to 2,995	3,000 or more
Minimum Point Value of First Meld:	50	90	120

Playing the Game

At the start of their turn, a player must draw two cards from the stock into their hand *or* take the entire discard pile. A player can only take the discard pile if they can *immediately* meld the top discard with two non-wild cards of the same rank from their hand. These can be added to existing melds or used to start a new one. If this is the first meld of the hand for the player's team and it doesn't meet the minimum points requirement, additional cards from the player's hand (not the discard pile) must be melded to meet the requirement. Once the minimum value has been achieved, the rest of the discard pile is added to the player's hand.

After drawing, a player may start new melds or add to their team's existing melds. When their turn is over, they must discard a single card and have at least one card remaining in their hand.

CONTINUED

Going Out

After drawing but before playing any cards in a turn (with the exception of red Threes drawn), a player may ask permission from their partner to "go out." If the partner agrees, the player plays every card in their hand. Discarding at the end of this turn is optional. By the end of the turn, the player's team must have melded at least one canasta.

"Going out concealed" happens when a player goes out without previously melding any cards. All rules for going out remain the same, including the requirement to ask their partner's permission. If their partner has not already melded, the player asking to go out must meet the points requirement for the first meld *and* meld an entire canasta.

Scoring

A hand ends when someone goes out or when the stock is used up and the next player can't take the discard pile. At this point, each team receives points as follows:

- **500 points** per natural canasta
- **300 points** per mixed canasta
- **100 points** per red Three (doubled if all four were played by the same team)
- **100 points** for going out (doubled if they went out concealed)
- **The total point value of *all* melded cards** (including those in canastas)

The total value of all cards remaining in a player's hand is *subtracted* from their team's score. When one or both teams reach 5,000 points, the team with the higher score wins.

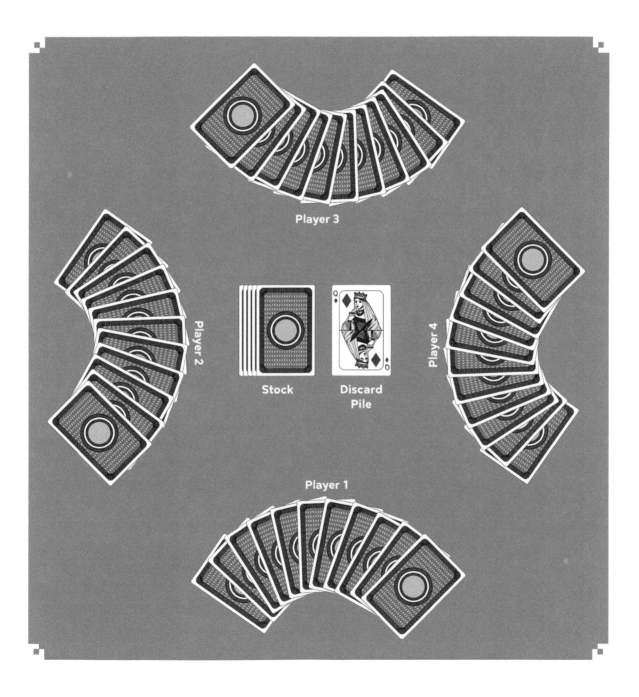

Player 3

Player 2

Stock

Discard
Pile

Player 4

Player 1

HAND AND FOOT

This expanded version of Canasta more than doubles the size of everything—including the fun!

OBJECTIVE: Have the highest score after five hands.

MATERIALS: 5 standard 52-card decks with Jokers, a scorekeeping method

Base Rules

Because so many rules overlap, we will only address points where Hand and Foot differs from ordinary Canasta (page 88).

Dealing

The dealer deals 13 cards to each player's hand. The player preceding the dealer deals 13 cards to each player's "foot," a secondary hand that is kept facedown until needed.

Card Properties

Red Threes are not played instantly; they are played at will during a player's turn. When one is played, two cards are drawn to replace it.

Melds

Canastas may not exceed seven cards. When one is completed, a team may start a new meld of the same rank. Melds containing only wild cards are permitted (however, a wild card on top of the discard pile still blocks it from being taken).

The minimum value of a team's first meld changes each hand:

Hand:	First	Second	Third	Fourth	Fifth
Minimum Value of First Meld:	50 points	90 points	120 points	150 points	1 full canasta (points irrelevant)

Playing the Game

Rules for drawing stock cards and taking the discard pile are the same. However, at the start of their turn, players may play red Threes from their hand *before drawing*. If the cards obtained from playing red Threes allow them to take the discard pile, they may do so.

When a player empties their hand, it's not considered "going out." Instead, they pick up their "foot" and use it as a second hand. This is called being "in their foot." If a player discards their final hand card, their turn is over; they may pick up their foot but can't play cards from it until their next turn. If they play their final hand card rather than discarding, they may pick up their foot and immediately play from it (because they haven't discarded, their turn has not ended). Aside from going out, a player in their foot may not discard their final card. If they have only one card remaining and don't meet the requirements for going out, they must keep it and say "pass the discard" to indicate that their turn is over.

Going Out

A player may not ask permission to go out unless both members of their team are "in their feet." When they have finished going out, their team must have at least one of each of the following melds:

- One natural canasta of Sevens

- One additional natural canasta

- One mixed canasta

- One wild canasta

Scoring

At the end of a hand, the team that went out (if any) receives 1,000 bonus points. Each team receives points for red Threes they played during the hand as follows:

- For playing **1 to 4 red Threes**, a team scores **100 points per red Three**.

- For playing **5 to 9 red Threes**, a team scores **1,000 points for the first five** (as a set, not each) and **100 points for each additional red Three**.

- For playing **all 10 red Threes**, a team scores **10,000 points for the whole set**.

CONTINUED

Each team receives points for melds they made during the hand as follows:

- **2,000 points** per wild canasta

- **1,500 points** per natural canasta of Sevens

- **1,000 points** per natural canasta of a rank other than Seven

- **300 points** per mixed canasta

- **The total point value of *all* melded cards** (including those in canastas)

The total value of all cards remaining in a player's hand and/or foot is *subtracted* from their team's score. After five hands, the team with the higher score wins.

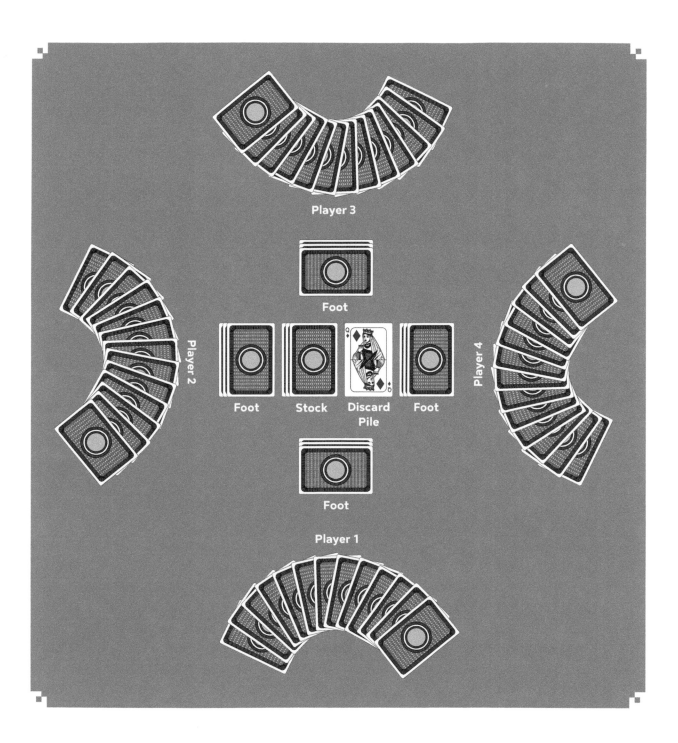

Player 3

Foot

Foot   Stock   Discard
                 Pile   Foot

Foot

Player 1

Player 2

Player 4

CRIBBAGE

Cribbage is a test of attention, mental math, and saying funny things when Jacks turn up.

OBJECTIVE: Be the first player to reach 121 points.

MATERIALS: One standard 52-card deck (no Jokers), a Cribbage board or alternate scorekeeping method

CARD RANKING: Ace = 1, face card = 10, number card = rank value

Setup

If using a Cribbage board, set pegs in the starting holes for each player.

Dealing

Deal six cards to each player's hand. Place the stock facedown on the table.

Playing the Game

After the deal, each player discards two cards facedown into a secondary hand for the dealer. This hand, called the "crib," is set aside until later. The nondealing player cuts the stock, and the dealer draws the top card from the bottom half. This is the "starter card"; it is placed faceup on top of the stock after the two parts are rejoined. If the starter card is a Jack, the dealer scores two points "for His Heels."

Next comes a phase called "the play," in which players take turns playing individual cards from their hands onto the table in front of them. (Each player will have their own pile of played cards; don't mix them!) The nondealer starts by playing a card and stating its numerical value. The dealer then plays a card and states the sum total of the cards played. This total is called the "count."

When a player is unable to play a card without the count exceeding 31, they say "go." The other player lays down any cards they can play on the current count without it exceeding 31. Then, the player who said "go" plays a card and starts a new count. If, at any point, only one player has cards remaining, they continue playing and building the count on their own until they are out of cards.

During the play, certain events and combinations score points for the player of the most recently played card. Combinations occur when a played card and the cards immediately preceding it *in the same count* form a set or run. An existing combination can be built into a larger combination by the next card. It doesn't matter who played the preceding cards as long as they were all played in the same count with no interruptions to the combination. Points are scored for all of the following:

Scoring "The Play"			
Category	**Description**	**Points Awarded**	**Notes**
Events	Played the last card of a count or hand.	1	For "the go" or "last card."
	Brought the count to exactly 15.	2	
	Brought the count to exactly 31.	2	No "go" or "last card" point awarded.
Combinations	Pair	2	
	Three of a kind	6	
Combinations (formed by the played card and cards immediately preceding it *in the same count*)	Four of a kind	12	
	Run of three or more	1 per card in the run	Suit is irrelevant. Can be played "out of order" (e.g., Nine, Seven, Eight).

After the play, both players gather their played cards for the next phase, called "the show." Both players look for every possible scoring combination that can be formed using the starter card and their four hand cards. The possible combinations are as follows:

CONTINUED

Scoring "The Show"		
Combination	**Points Awarded**	**Notes**
Fifteen	2	Any group of cards totaling 15 in numerical value.
Pair	2	Three of a kind forms three unique pairs (6 points); four of a kind forms six unique pairs (12 points).
Run of three or more	1 per card	Suit is irrelevant.
Four-card flush	4	Formed using hand cards *without* the starting card. Not valid in the crib.
Five-card flush	5	Valid in both hand and crib.
Jack of the same suit as the starter card	1	"For His Nobs."

Cards may be reused in different combinations, including multiple combinations of the same type. The nondealer scores their points first, followed by the dealer. The dealer then turns up the crib and scores it in the same way, adding the points to their total.

Whenever a player scores points, they are immediately counted toward the player's total for the game. Regardless of what phase of a hand they're in, a player wins as soon as they score their 121st point.

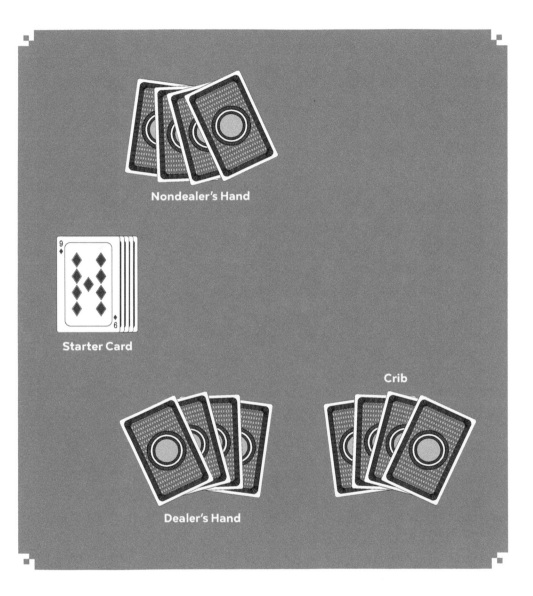

Nondealer's Hand

Starter Card

Crib

Dealer's Hand

CHAPTER 4

PATIENCE
GAMES

PYRAMID

Rumor has it the ancient pharaohs would have played this game if it had existed at the time.

OBJECTIVE: Discard every card from the tableau.

NUMERICAL CARD VALUES: Ace = 1, Jack = 11, Queen = 12, King = 13, number card = rank value

MATERIALS: One standard 52-card deck (no Jokers)

Tableau Layout

The tableau resembles a pyramid containing 28 faceup cards in seven overlapping rows. The top row contains a single card. Each row that follows contains one more card than, and starts half a card-width to the left of, the previous row. Every card in the top six rows should be partly covered by the corners of two cards in the following row.

Place the stock faceup below the tableau. At any time, the top card of the stock can be moved to a second faceup pile called the "waste." (Note: This is *not* where matched cards are discarded.)

Playing the Game

Any two exposed cards whose numerical values add up to 13 may be picked up and discarded together. Exposed cards include fully uncovered tableau cards and the top cards of the stock and waste. Exposed Kings, which count as 13 on their own, may be discarded individually. When the stock is empty, reverse the order of the waste cards and place them back in the stock. This can be done up to two times. If the player succeeds in emptying the tableau before running out of valid moves, the game is won.

Stock

TRI PEAKS

Created in 1989, this game is named for the shape of its tableau, which resembles three mountain peaks.

OBJECTIVE: Discard every card from the tableau.

MATERIALS: One standard 52-card deck (no Jokers)

CARD RANKING: Natural, Aces treated as both high and low

Tableau Layout

The tableau contains 28 cards in four rows:

1. **First Row:** Three facedown cards with a two-card gap after the first and second cards.

2. **Second Row:** Six facedown cards with a one-card gap after the second and fourth cards.

3. **Third Row:** Nine facedown cards in a continuous row.

4. **Fourth Row:** Ten faceup cards in a continuous row.

Each row partly overlaps, and starts half a card-width to the left of, the previous row. Place the stock facedown below the tableau and turn up the top card beside it to start a faceup discard pile.

Playing the Game

One at a time, the player may discard any faceup card in the tableau that is one rank above or below the top card of the discard pile. When a facedown card is completely uncovered, it is turned up. The top card of the stock may be turned up onto the discard pile at any time. If the player succeeds in emptying the tableau before the stock is exhausted and no valid moves remain, the game is won.

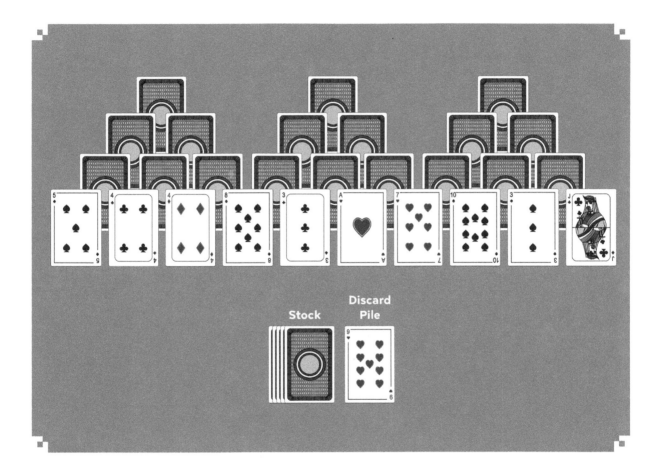

Stock

Discard Pile

FREECELL

1 PLAYER   **MEDIUM** | **LENGTH OF PLAY:** 5 TO 20 MINUTES

Unlike in most patience games, very few (fewer than 1 in 100,000) FreeCell layouts are unsolvable.

OBJECTIVE: Sort all cards into four foundation piles, each containing an entire suit arranged in ascending order.

MATERIALS: One standard 52-card deck (no Jokers)

CARD RANKING: Natural, Aces low

Tableau Layout

Deal eight piles in a horizontal row with all cards faceup. From left to right, the first four piles contain seven cards each. The remaining piles contain six cards each. Fan the piles into columns so card ranks and suits are visible. Imagine that there is an empty, card-size space above each of the eight columns. Foundation piles (which start empty) will be placed in the four rightmost spaces. The four leftmost spaces are called "free cells"; each of these can be used during the game to temporarily hold any card.

Playing the Game

Exposed tableau cards (those with no other cards on top of them) and cards in free cells can be moved to one of four places:

- ◆ Onto an exposed tableau card that is one rank higher and a different color (i.e., built down by alternating color)

- ◆ To an empty free cell

- ◆ To an empty column

- ◆ To a foundation pile, if it is the next card in sequence for its foundation pile

Foundation piles are started by moving Aces to empty foundation pile spaces. Cards placed on foundation piles may not be removed from them. Once all four Kings have been placed, the game is won.

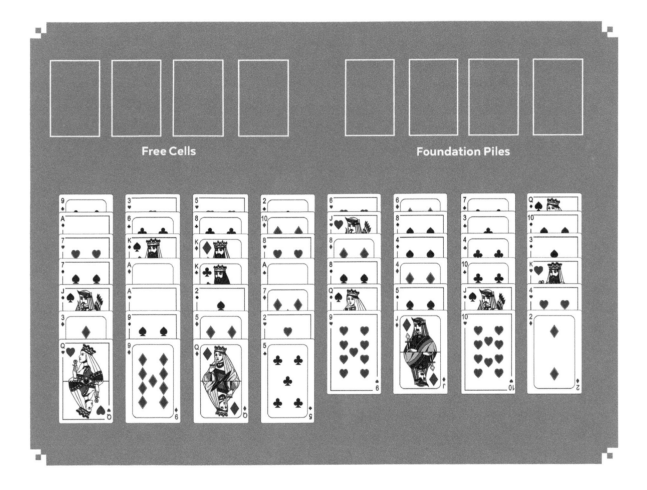

Free Cells

Foundation Piles

KLONDIKE (CLASSIC SOLITAIRE)

1 PLAYER   **MEDIUM** | **LENGTH OF PLAY:** 10 TO 30 MINUTES

Klondike is such a well-known patience/solitaire game that it is often just called Patience or Solitaire.

OBJECTIVE: Sort all cards into four foundation piles, each containing an entire suit in ascending order.

MATERIALS: One standard 52-card deck (no Jokers)

CARD RANKING: Natural, Aces low

Tableau Layout

Deal seven piles of cards in a horizontal row. All cards are facedown except the top card of each pile. The leftmost pile contains a single card; from left to right, each pile contains one more card than the previous pile. Fan the piles into columns to easily see how many cards are in each.

The foundation piles (which start empty) will be placed above the four rightmost columns of the tableau. Traditionally, the stock is placed above the leftmost column. (We find this placement awkward; you may find it easier to hold the stock or place it below the tableau.)

Playing the Game

To complete the objective, the player must reveal all downturned cards in the tableau and retrieve every card from the stock. Facedown tableau cards may not be moved. When one is exposed (all cards on top of it are removed), it is turned up and available for play.

Cards may be moved according to the following rules:

♦ **Drawing:** At any time, the top three cards of the stock may be turned up and placed beside it in a faceup "waste" pile. If fewer than three stock cards remain, turn up all remaining cards. The player may know the values of all waste cards (it's common to fan the top three) and the top card of the waste pile is available to be drawn. When the stock is empty, it can be refreshed by squaring the waste and turning it facedown (without shuffling) to form a new stock.

- **Building Down:** The top card of the waste pile or any exposed card in the tableau may be moved onto an exposed tableau card that is one rank higher and a different color. All or part of an existing built-down column can be moved in this way; the top-ranked card of the moved sequence must be one rank lower and a different color than the card on which it is placed.

- **Filling an Empty Column:** If a column is empty, a King (along with any cards built down on top of it) may be moved into the empty space.

- **Moving to Foundations:** The top card of the waste pile or any tableau column may be moved to a foundation pile if it is the next card in sequence for its foundation pile (one rank higher than the current top card). Foundation piles are started by placing an Ace in an empty foundation pile slot. Once all four Kings have been placed, the game is won.

Variations

- **Multiplayer:** See Double Klondike (page 114) and Nerts (page 111).

- **Draw 1:** Turn up one stock card instead of three.

- **Limited Passes:** The stock may be refreshed a limited number of times (usually twice).

- **Unbreakable Columns:** No splitting of built-down columns.

- **Scoring/Timekeeping:** Common in electronic versions of Klondike.

CONTINUED

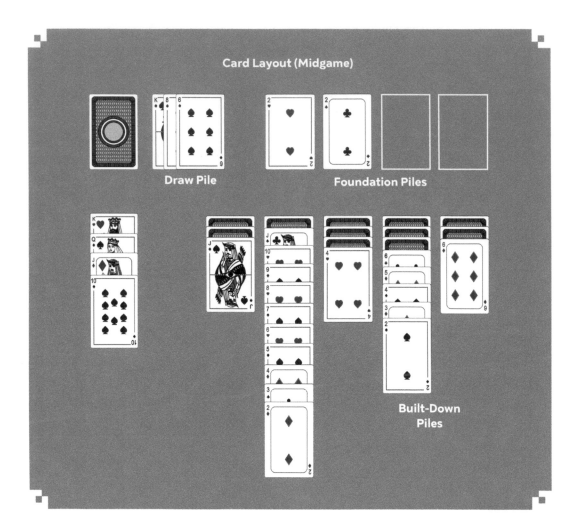

Card Layout (Midgame)

Draw Pile

Foundation Piles

Built-Down Piles

NERTS

Also called Pounce and sometimes spelled Nertz, this game is a mix of Double Klondike (page 114), Speed (page 64), and Spit (page 58).

OBJECTIVE: Be the first player to reach 100 points.

MATERIALS: One standard 52-card deck *per player*, each with a different back (no Jokers)

CARD RANKING: Natural, Aces low

Tableau Layout

Each player uses their own deck and deals their own tableau, which has three parts:

- ◆ **River:** Four cards dealt faceup in a horizontal row.

- ◆ **Nerts Pile:** A pile of 13 cards beside the river. All cards are facedown except the top card.

- ◆ **Stream:** The stock (placed facedown) and a waste pile that will be started beside it. These are kept below the river.

The common area between the tableaus is called **the lake**.

Playing the Game

All players start playing at the same time, using only one hand and moving one card at a time. Any uncovered, faceup card in the river, stream, or nerts pile can be moved. When the top card of a nerts pile is removed, the next card is immediately turned up.

The top three cards of the stock can be turned faceup on the waste pile at any time. If fewer than three remain, turn up all remaining cards. The player may know the values of all waste cards (it's common to fan the top three). An empty stock can be refreshed by squaring the waste and turning it facedown (without shuffling) to form a new stock.

CONTINUED

A card may be moved to or within the river by placing it on an exposed (uncovered) card that is one rank higher and a different color. The resulting piles should be fanned into columns so that the card ranks and suits can be seen. Multiple cards from the top of a pile (the lower-ranked cards of a column) can be moved as a unit from one river column to another as long as the top-ranked card of the moved sequence is one rank lower and a different color than the card on which it is placed. Any available card or movable river column sequence may be placed in an empty river slot.

A "foundation pile" contains an entire suit in ascending order (Ace on the bottom, King on the top). Foundation piles are started by playing an Ace into the lake. Any player can play cards onto any existing foundation pile. If multiple players try to play on the same foundation pile at once, the card that touched the pile first is considered played; the others must return to where they came from.

When a player's nerts pile is empty, they may call "Nerts!" and end the hand. However, they're not required to do so immediately. The hand ends automatically if all players run out of legal moves. At the end of a hand, players receive one point for each card played to the lake, 10 points for being the first to call "Nerts," and –2 points for each card remaining in their nerts piles. The first player to reach 100 total points wins.

Lake

River

Stream

Nerts Pile

DOUBLE KLONDIKE

2 PLAYERS   **MEDIUM** | **LENGTH OF PLAY:** 5 TO 15 MINUTES

It's no wonder that somebody invented a two-player version of the most popular patience game in the world. For a similar game that can include even more players, check out Nerts (page 111).

OBJECTIVE: Play more cards to foundation piles than your opponent.

MATERIALS: Two standard 52-card decks with different backs (no Jokers)

CARD RANKING: Natural, Aces low

Playing the Game

In terms of game play, Double Klondike is almost identical to ordinary Klondike (page 108). The major difference is that two players play simultaneously, sharing eight foundation piles between them.

Each player uses their own deck. Sitting opposite each other, they each deal a standard Klondike tableau. When both are ready, they start playing at the same time, using only one hand and moving one card at a time. Either player can start or build upon any of the eight foundation piles, which are placed between the tableaus where both players can reach them. If both players try to play on the same foundation pile at once, the card that touched the pile first is considered played; the other must return to where it came from.

If one player empties their tableau into foundation piles, they win instantly. Otherwise, the game ends when both players have run out of legal moves. Whoever played more cards into foundation piles is the winner.

Foundation Area

Tableau ———————————————— Stack

SPIDER

Supposedly, this game was named for the fact that you need to make eight foundation piles. Other than that, there's nothing spiderlike about it—aside from the fact that you sometimes feel caught in a web.

OBJECTIVE: Sort all cards into eight foundation piles, each containing an entire suit arranged in rank order.

MATERIALS: Two standard 52-card decks (no Jokers)

CARD RANKING: Natural, Aces low

Setup

Shuffle the decks together.

Tableau Layout

Deal 10 piles of cards in a horizontal row. All cards are facedown except the top card of each pile. From left to right, the first four piles contain six cards each. The remaining piles contain five cards each. Fan the piles into columns to easily see how many cards are in each. Keep the stock below the tableau, within reach of the player.

Playing the Game

To complete the objective, the player must reveal all downturned cards in the tableau and retrieve every card from the stock. Facedown tableau cards may not be moved. When one is exposed (all cards on top of it are removed), it is turned up and available for play.

An exposed tableau card may be moved onto another exposed card if it is one rank lower than the card on which it is placed. In other words, tableau columns may be built down in descending sequences. The cards in a built-down sequence can be of different suits; however, a sequence made up of only one suit has an advantage in that it can be moved like a single card. This includes suit sequences that make up the bottom portions of larger sequences. As long as it's not blocked in by other cards, a suit sequence of any length (including just two cards) can be moved and placed on an exposed card that is one rank higher than its top-ranked card.

Empty columns in the tableau can be filled with movable cards or suit sequences. (This is the only possible destination for a King or a suit sequence built on a King.) Whenever there are no empty columns, the player may opt to deal additional cards to the tableau from the stock. This is done by placing one card from the stock faceup on each of the 10 columns. Because the stock has 50 cards, this must be done five times throughout the game.

Any time a 13-card suit sequence (King down to Ace, all of the same suit) is created in the tableau, it is removed and becomes one of the eight foundation piles. When the stock and tableau are empty and eight foundation piles have been created, the game is won.

Variations

♦ **Two-Suit Game (Medium Difficulty):** Choose two suits. Retrieve all cards belonging to those suits from four different decks. Shuffle them together and play as normal.

♦ **One-Suit Game (Easy Difficulty):** Choose one suit. Retrieve all cards belonging to that suit from eight different decks. Shuffle them together and play as normal.

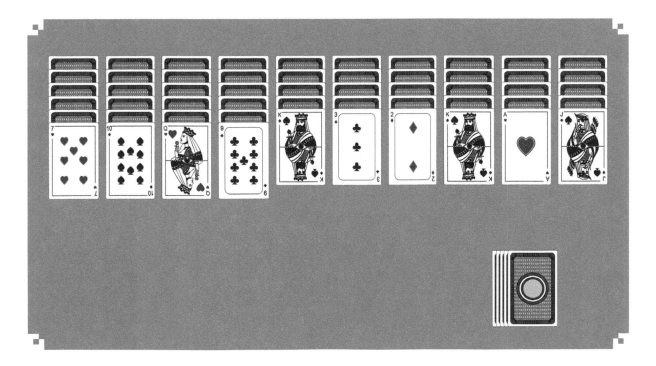

ST. HELENA

Not to be confused with Napoleon at St. Helena, a variation of the game Emperor (page 121), this game is also called Napoleon's Favorite or Washington's Favorite.

OBJECTIVE: Sort all cards into eight foundation piles, each containing an entire suit arranged in ascending or descending order.

MATERIALS: Two standard 52-card decks (no Jokers)

CARD RANKING: Natural, Aces low

Tableau Layout

From one deck, retrieve all Kings and Aces. (If the decks are already mixed, take one King and Ace of each suit.) Place the Kings faceup in a horizontal row. Below them, place the Aces in a second row, forming a grid of two rows by four columns. These are the beginnings of the foundation piles.

Shuffle the remaining cards together. These will be dealt into 12 "border piles" containing eight cards each. Border piles are situated above and below each column and on either side of each row, surrounding the foundation piles. Starting above the top-left King and moving clockwise, deal one faceup card to each of the 12 positions. Repeat until the piles are complete.

Playing the Game

The top card of any border pile is available to be moved. An available card can be moved to another border pile where the top card's rank is one higher or one lower than its own (suit irrelevant). If a border pile slot becomes empty, the space may be filled by an Ace or King from a different border pile.

An available card can be placed on a foundation pile that matches its suit when it is the next card in sequence for that foundation pile. All foundation piles are built sequentially by rank, but piles of the same suit go in opposite directions. The ones in the top row are built in *descending* order (King down to Ace). The other four are built in *ascending* order (Ace up to King). Cards may not be removed from foundation piles.

At the start of the game, there are restrictions on which border piles can play to which foundation piles. Cards from the top four border piles can only be played to the top row of foundation piles. Likewise, the bottom border piles can only play to the bottom foundation piles. The border piles on the sides have no restrictions. After the first redeal (see below), all of the restrictions are lifted.

Redealing

The player is allowed to redeal twice during the game. This is done to refresh the tableau when they have run out of legal moves. First, the border piles are stacked in sequential order with the first pile in deal order on the bottom and the 12th pile on top. Kept faceup and unshuffled, the cards are dealt as before. (If cards have been moved to foundation piles, some or all of the border piles will have fewer than eight cards.) If the player manages to move every card to a foundation pile before running out of legal moves after the second redeal, the game is won.

CONTINUED

EMPEROR

1 PLAYER   **HARD** | **LENGTH OF PLAY:** 15 TO 20 MINUTES

Emperor changes up the solitaire format by forcing you to build tableau columns in reverse.

OBJECTIVE: Sort all cards into eight foundation piles, each containing an entire suit arranged in ascending order.

MATERIALS: Two standard 52-card decks (no Jokers)

CARD RANKING: Natural, Aces low

Tableau Layout

Deal 10 piles, each containing four cards, in a horizontal row. All cards are facedown except the top card of each pile. Fan the piles into columns to easily see how many cards are in each.

The foundation piles (which start empty) will be placed above the tableau. Place the stock facedown below the tableau.

Playing the Game

Emperor is played almost exactly like Klondike (page 108) with the following differences:

♦ Tableau columns are built *up* instead of down. Cards are placed on exposed cards that are a different color and one rank *lower*.

♦ Only one tableau card may be moved at a time (no stack movement).

♦ Any available card may be placed in an empty column.

♦ Only one stock card is turned up at a time. The stock is not refreshed when empty. Optionally, the entire waste pile may be fanned.

Variation

♦ **Forty Thieves/Napoleon at St. Helena:** All tableau cards start faceup. Tableau columns are built down by suit (cards are placed on cards of the same suit that are one rank higher).

CONTINUED

Foundation Piles

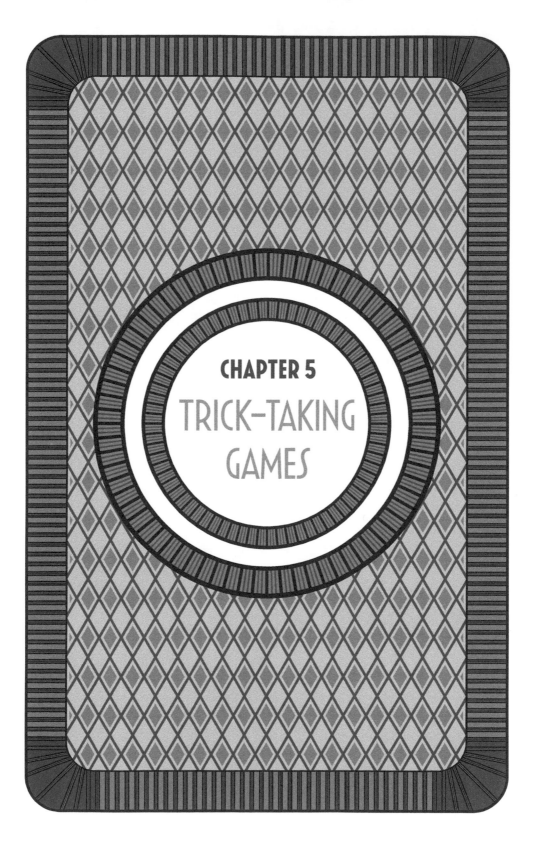

CHAPTER 5

TRICK-TAKING GAMES

WHIST

A predecessor to Hearts (page 128), Spades (page 152), and Bridge (page 133), Whist is a good introduction to trick-taking games. If you're new to trick-taking games, please see the brief overview on page 11.

OBJECTIVE: Be the first team to reach 5 points.

MATERIALS: One standard 52-card deck (no Jokers), a second deck for swapping out between hands (optional), Whist markers or an alternate scorekeeping method

CARD RANKING: Natural, Aces high; with trump suit

Setup

Players pair up in teams of two. Teammates sit opposite each other.

Traditionally, Whist is played with two decks that are swapped between hands. The dealer's partner shuffles the deck used for the previous hand while the dealer deals the current hand. This is a time-saving measure and is completely optional.

Dealing

Deal 13 cards to each player's hand. The last card dealt to the dealer is turned faceup on the table. This card's suit is the trump suit for the hand. On the dealer's first turn, they may place this card in their hand.

Playing the Game

A hand is played in a series of 13 tricks. The starting player leads the first trick. Everyone else plays to the trick in turn and must follow suit if possible. If a player cannot follow suit, they may play any other card from their hand. Whoever played the highest-ranking card of the led suit takes the trick unless one or more trump cards were played, in which case the highest-ranking trump card wins the trick. The player who takes a trick leads the next trick of the hand.

Scoring

At the end of a hand, points are awarded for tricks taken. The first six tricks taken by a team are worth nothing; each trick taken after the sixth is worth one point. When at least one team has reached 5 points, the team with the higher score wins. (If the score is tied, play a tiebreaker hand.)

Variations

- **American Whist:** Play to 7 points.

- **Long Whist:** Play to 9 points.

- **Tournament Rules:** Instead of being selected randomly, the trump suit for each hand is predetermined, rotating between Hearts, Diamonds, Spades, and Clubs, in that order. Sometimes, the fifth hand in the cycle has no trump suit.

HEARTS

This version is actually a variation of the original Hearts that has surpassed the original's popularity. If you're new to trick-taking games, please see the brief overview on page 11.

OBJECTIVE: Have the lowest score when another player reaches 100 points.

MATERIALS: One standard 52-card deck (no Jokers), a scorekeeping method

CARD RANKING: Natural, Aces high

Dealing

Deal 13 cards to each player's hand.

The Passing Phase

At the start of most hands, each player selects three cards from their hand to pass (face-down) to another player. The passing rules change on a four-hand cycle as follows:

- **First Hand:** Pass to the next player.

- **Second Hand:** Pass to the previous player.

- **Third Hand:** Pass to the player directly across the table.

- **Fourth Hand:** No passing; everyone keeps their dealt cards.

Playing the Game

A hand is played in a series of 13 tricks. The player who holds the Two of Clubs uses it to lead the first trick. Everyone else plays to the trick in turn and must follow suit if possible. If a player cannot follow suit, they may play any other card from their hand. Whoever played the highest-ranking card *of the led suit* takes the trick and leads the next trick of the hand.

Scoring cards include all Heart cards, which are worth 1 point each, and the Queen of Spades, which is worth 13 points. Unless a player was dealt only scoring cards (incredibly unlikely), scoring cards may not be played during the first trick of a hand. Unless a player has only Heart cards, Hearts may not be played as the led suit of a trick until Hearts has been "broken" in a hand. Hearts are broken when a Heart card is played on a trick where Hearts was not the led suit.

At the end of each hand, players receive points for the scoring cards they've taken in tricks. This amount is added to their total score for the game. However, if one player took all of the scoring cards, they have "shot the moon." This player can either subtract 26 points from their own score or add 26 points to every other player's score. When one player reaches a total score of 100, the player with the lowest score wins.

Variations

♦ Accommodate more or fewer players with the following rule adjustments:

  ♦ **Three Players:** Remove the Two of Diamonds. Deal each player 17 cards. Eliminate the "pass across" phase.

  ♦ **Five Players:** Remove the Two of Diamonds and Two of Clubs. Three of Clubs becomes the starting card. Deal each player 10 cards. Eliminate the "pass across" phase.

  ♦ **Six Players:** Remove the Two and Three of Diamonds and the Three and Four of Clubs. Deal each player 8 cards.

  ♦ **Seven Players:** Remove the Two and Three of Diamonds and the Three of Clubs. Deal each player 7 cards. Eliminate the "pass across" phase.

KNACK

This Swedish game is thought to have developed from an old Danish game called Trekort, meaning "three cards." If you're new to trick-taking games, please see the brief overview on page 11.

MATERIALS: One standard 52-card deck (no Jokers), betting chips

CARD RANKING: Natural, Aces high

Setup

Remove all Twos, Threes, Fours, and Fives from the deck. Distribute betting chips to each player and decide on a stake amount that's divisible by three. The exact numbers don't matter, but you'll want to make sure each player has enough chips to participate in a sufficient number of hands.

Dealing

Deal three cards to each player's hand. Turn up the next card off the stock; this card's suit is the trump suit for the hand. Any player who wishes may discard up to two cards from their hand and receive replacements from the stock.

Betting

The dealer bets the agreed-upon stake amount into the pot. In turn, all players (including the dealer) decide whether to play the hand (traditionally announced by knocking on the table) or fold, meaning they will sit the hand out. If all but one player folds, the remaining player automatically wins the pot and the hand ends.

Playing the Game

A hand is played in a series of three tricks. The starting player leads the first trick and must lead with the Ace of the trump suit if possible. The leader of the second trick must lead with any trump card if possible. In both cases, if a player doesn't have the necessary card(s), they may lead with any card from their hand. (There is no lead requirement for the third trick.)

After the trick has been led, everyone else plays to the trick in turn and must follow suit if possible. If a player cannot follow suit, they may play any other card from their hand. Whoever played the highest-ranking card of the led suit takes the trick unless one or more trump cards were played, in which case the highest-ranking trump card wins the trick. The player who takes a trick leads the next trick of the hand.

At the end of a hand, any player who played but failed to take any tricks pays the stake amount into the pot. The remaining players win one-third of the pot for each trick taken. Play for a set number of hands or until all but one player is out of chips. Whoever has the most chips at the end wins.

Variation

Köpknack is a similar game with the following differences:

+ Players exchange cards from their hand *after* deciding to play or fold and may do so two times. They may exchange up to three cards each time.

+ The first trick may be led with any trump card.

+ If a player is unable to follow suit, they *must* play a trump card if possible.

+ A player who plays a hand but failed to take any tricks pays a double stake into the pot.

CONTINUED

BRIDGE

Contract Bridge, usually shortened to Bridge, is one of the most popular card games in the world. This version is Rubber Bridge, common for casual play; competitive Bridge has slightly different rules. This game is particularly complex; if you're a beginner, don't be discouraged if you have trouble understanding it. If you're new to trick-taking games, please see the brief overview on page 11.

OBJECTIVE: Score the most points over the course of three games.

MATERIALS: One standard 52-card deck (no Jokers), a method for recording scores and bids

CARD RANKING: Natural, Aces high; with trump suit

Setup

Players pair up in teams of two. Teammates sit opposite each other. Traditionally, the four player positions (moving clockwise around the table) are called North, East, South, and West. North is the first dealer.

Dealing

Deal 13 cards to each player's hand.

Bidding

After looking at their hands, players bid to become the "declarer." Bids are stated out loud in the form of a number plus either a suit or a "no trump" declaration. The number represents how many tricks *above six* the bidder is committing their team to win during the hand.

During the bid, suits have an ascending order of Clubs, Diamonds, Hearts, and Spades, with "no trump" outranking every suit. Players can beat previous bids by declaring the same number with a higher-ranking suit declaration.

CONTINUED

Beginning with the starting player, each player in turn must make an initial bid, raise on a previous bid, or pass. If all players pass without bidding, the hand ends in a misdeal. Players may bid even if they've passed previously.

If the current bid was made by the opposing team, a player may declare "double" in lieu of bidding or passing. This keeps the current bid in place but doubles the points won by either team at the end of the hand. On their next turn, either member of the opposing team may declare "redouble," which doubles the points again. Doubles and redoubles are canceled if anyone makes a higher bid.

Bidding ends when three players in a row pass, or when "Seven no trump" (the highest possible bid) is redoubled. The suit attached to the bid becomes the trump suit for the hand ("no trump" means there is no trump suit). Of the partners on the bid-winning team, the one who *first* called the winning suit in a bid becomes the declarer.

Playing the Game

The player after the declarer in turn order leads the first trick. Everyone else plays to the trick in turn and must follow suit if possible. If they can't, they may play any card from their hand. Whoever played the highest-ranking card of the led suit takes the trick unless one or more trump cards were played, in which case the highest-ranking trump card wins the trick. The player who takes a trick leads the next trick of the hand.

On their first turn, the declarer's partner lays their hand faceup and sits out the remainder of the hand. The declarer plays from this "dummy hand" during the turn that would normally belong to their partner.

Scoring

Bridge is played in a series of three games called a "rubber." There are two types of points (whose names reference the layout of a typical Bridge scorecard): "above-the-line" points and "contract" (or "below-the-line") points. Both types contribute to the overall score for the rubber; however, a team must score 100 *contract points* to win a game. Contract points in excess of 100 count toward overall score for the rubber but *don't* count toward winning the next game.

A team that has won a game is declared "vulnerable." When a team has won two games, the team with the higher score wins. Points for a hand are awarded as follows:

Points for Meeting the Bid			
Trump Suit	Clubs or Diamonds	Hearts or Spades	No Trump
Contract Points (Awarded to Declarer)	20 times bid amount	30 times bid amount	30 times bid amount plus 10 bonus points

All amounts x2 if bid was doubled, x4 if redoubled.

Points for Overtricks (Tricks Taken in Excess of Bid)							
Bid Status	Not Doubled			Doubled		Redoubled	
Trump Suit	Clubs or Diamonds	Hearts or Spades	No Trump	Any			
Is Declarer Vulnerable?	Irrelevant			No	Yes	No	Yes
Above-the-Line Points per Overtrick (Awarded to Declarer)	20	30	30	100	200	200	400

Penalty for Failing to Meet the Bid							
Bid Status		Not Doubled		Doubled		Redoubled	
Is Declarer Vulnerable?		No	Yes	No	Yes	No	Yes
Above-the-Line Points (Awarded to Declarer's Opponents)	**First Undertrick**	50	100	100	200	200	400
	Each Additional Undertrick	50	100	200	300	400	600

CONTINUED

Bonus Points		
Event	**Description**	**Above-the-Line Points Awarded**
Small Slam	Met a bid of 6	500 if not vulnerable, 750 if vulnerable
Grand Slam	Met a bid of 7	1,000 if not vulnerable, 1,500 if vulnerable
Insult Bonus	Met a doubled or redoubled bid	50 for doubled, 100 for redoubled
Slow Rubber	Won two games when opponents have won one	500
Fast Rubber	Won two games when opponents have won none	700
Honor Bonus	Hand contains 4 or 5 honor cards (Ace, King, Queen, Jack, & Ten of trump suit)	100 for four, 150 for all five
No-Trump Honor Bonus	Hand contains all four Aces in a "no trump" hand	150

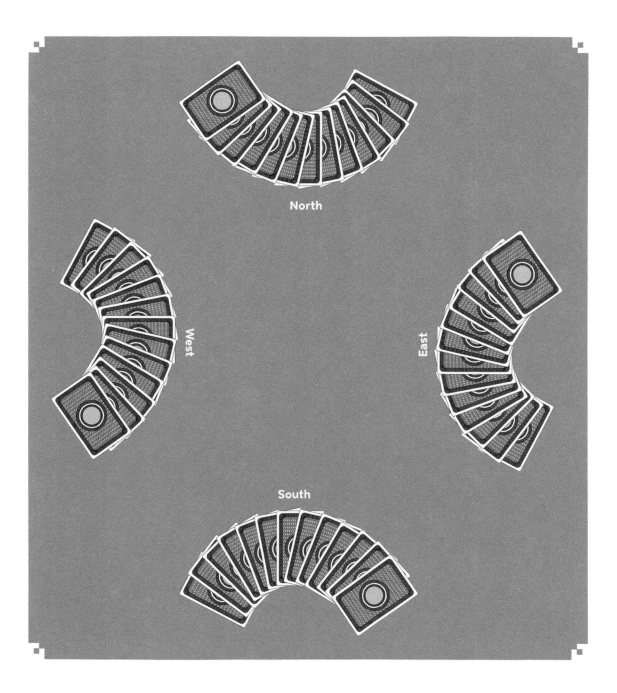

North

West

East

South

BLACKOUT

This game has some colorful alternative names that make us wish we could have been there the first time it was played: "Oh Hell," "Oh Pshaw," and "Oh! Well." If you're new to trick-taking games, please see the brief overview on page 11.

OBJECTIVE: Have the highest score after a set number of hands.

MATERIALS: One standard 52-card deck (no Jokers)

CARD RANKING: Natural, Aces high; with trump suit

Dealing

Unlike many trick-taking games, Blackout is played over a set number of hands, each consisting of an increasing number of tricks. In the first hand, each player is dealt one card (consequently, the hand consists of a single trick). In each hand that follows, players are dealt one more card than in the previous hand. The total number of hands depends on the number of players:

Number of Players	2	3	4	5	6	7
Number of Hands	18	15	13	10	8	7

In all but the final hand of the game, the dealer turns up the top card of the stock after dealing. This card's suit is the trump suit for the hand. The final hand is played without a trump suit.

Playing the Game

After looking at their dealt cards, each player in turn bids a number of tricks they think they'll take during the hand. The bid must be between zero and the number of cards in their hand. The starting player leads the first trick. Everyone else plays to the trick in turn and must follow suit if possible. If a player cannot follow suit, they may play any card from their hand. Whoever played the highest-ranking card of the led suit takes the trick unless one or more cards of the trump suit were played, in which case the highest-ranking trump card wins the trick. The player who takes a trick leads the next trick of the hand.

At the end of a hand, if a player took exactly as many tricks as they bid, they win 10 points plus the bid amount. If they are over or under their bid, they win zero points. The score for the hand is added to their total score for the game. After all hands have been played, the player with the highest total score wins.

FORTY-FIVES

2 TO 6 PLAYERS | **HARD** | **LENGTH OF PLAY:** 10 TO 20 MINUTES

This game was named for the number of headache pills you have to take while playing it. If you're new to trick-taking games, please see the brief overview on page 11.

OBJECTIVE: Be the first player to reach 45 points.

MATERIALS: One standard 52-card deck (no Jokers)

CARD RANKING: Yikes. So, the Ace of Hearts is *always* the third-highest trump card. Everything else depends on which suit is the trump suit:

Suit	├─── Descending Rank Order ───▶				
Trump Suit Rankings						
♥	5 ♥	J ♥	A ♥	K ♥	Q ♥	10 ♥
♦	5 ♦	J ♦	A ♥	A ♦	K ♦	Q ♦
♣	5 ♣	J ♣	A ♥	A ♣	K ♣	Q ♣
♠	5 ♠	J ♠	A ♥	A ♠	K ♠	Q ♠
Nontrump Suit Rankings						
♥	K ♥	Q ♥	J ♥	10 ♥	9 ♥	8 ♥
♦	K ♦	Q ♦	J ♦	10 ♦	9 ♦	8 ♦
♣	K ♣	Q ♣	J ♣	A ♣	2 ♣	3 ♣
♠	K ♠	Q ♠	J ♠	A ♠	2 ♠	3 ♠

			Descending Rank Order ⟶				
Trump Suit Rankings							
9♥	8♥	7♥	6♥	4♥	3♥	2♥	
10♦	9♦	8♦	7♦	6♦	4♦	3♦	2♦
2♣	3♣	4♣	6♣	7♣	8♣	9♣	10♣
2♠	3♠	4♠	6♠	7♠	8♠	9♠	10♠
Nontrump Suit Rankings							
7♥	6♥	5♥	4♥	3♥	2♥		
7♦	6♦	5♦	4♦	3♦	2♦	A♦	
4♣	5♣	6♣	7♣	8♣	9♣	10♣	
4♠	5♠	6♠	7♠	8♠	9♠	10♠	

CONTINUED

Dealing

Deal five cards to each player's hand, giving each a batch of three followed by a batch of two. Turn up the next card off the stock; this card's suit is the trump suit for the hand. If it's an Ace, the dealer may claim it by discarding a card from their hand; it remains on the table until after the first trick, at which point the dealer places it in their hand.

If any player was dealt the trump Ace, they must swap the turned-up card for any card in their hand or ask the dealer to turn it facedown. If they do neither, thus hiding that they hold the trump Ace, it becomes the *lowest* trump card.

Playing the Game

The starting player leads the first trick. Everyone else plays to the trick in turn and must follow suit if possible. If they can't, they must play a trump card if possible. If they don't have a trump card, they may play any other card. Whoever played the highest-ranking card of the led suit takes the trick unless one or more trump cards were played, in which case the highest-ranking trump card wins the trick. The winner of a trick leads the next.

If the trump suit is led, players are not required to follow suit with the three highest-ranking trump cards (trump Five, trump Jack, and Ace of Hearts) but must play another trump card if they have one. If the Ace of Hearts is led, the trump suit is the led suit, and a player who can't or needn't play a trump card must play a Heart if possible.

At the end of a hand, each player gains five points for every trick they took during the hand. If trumps were played, whoever played the highest trump card wins five bonus points. The first player to reach 45 total points wins.

EUCHRE

4 PLAYERS   **HARD** | **LENGTH OF PLAY:** 20 TO 30 MINUTES

Popular throughout the English-speaking world, Euchre was once considered America's national card game. If you're new to trick-taking games, please see the brief overview on page 11.

OBJECTIVE: Be the first team to reach 10 points.

MATERIALS: One standard 52-card deck (no Jokers)

CARD RANKING: The highest-ranking card is the Jack of the trump suit, followed by the nontrump Jack of the same color as the trump suit (this card is treated as part of the trump suit). The remaining trump cards in descending order are Ace, King, Queen, Ten, and Nine. Nontrump cards (minus the Jack whose color matches the trump suit) are ranked naturally, Aces high.

Setup

Remove the Eights, Sevens, Sixes, Fives, Fours, Threes, and Twos from the deck. Players pair up in teams of two. Teammates sit opposite each other.

Dealing

Deal five cards to each player's hand, giving each a batch of three followed by a batch of two. A player who is dealt only Nines and Tens may request a redeal. Place the remaining cards facedown and turn up the top card.

Playing the Game

Beginning with the starting player, each player says "pick it up" or "pass" to indicate whether or not they want the suit of the turned-up card to be the trump suit for the hand. If any player says "pick it up," the dealer discards one card from their hand and takes the turned-up card. The card's suit becomes the trump suit. If all players pass, the card is turned facedown and each player in turn may name a different suit or pass. The first suit named becomes the trump suit. If all players pass, the hand ends in a misdeal.

CONTINUED

Regardless of how the trump suit was chosen, the team of the player who chose it is the "attackers." The other team is the "defenders." By naming the trump suit, a player asserts that their team will win the majority of the tricks in the hand. If they fail to do so, their opponents will win double points. If the player who chose trump believes they can win without their partner's help, they may indicate they wish to "go alone," which is worth bonus points if they take every trick. Their partner lays down their cards and sits out the hand.

The starting player leads the first trick. Everyone else plays to the trick in turn and must follow suit if possible. If they can't follow suit, they may play any card from their hand. Whoever played the highest-ranking card of the led suit takes the trick unless one or more trump cards were played, in which case the highest-ranking trump card wins the trick. The player who takes a trick leads the next trick of the hand.

At the end of each hand, points are awarded as follows:

Scoring Table				
Tricks Captured by Attackers	0	1-2	3-4	5
Points Earned by Attackers	0	0	1	2 normally, 4 if attacker "went alone"
Points Earned by Defenders	4	2	0	0

The first team to reach 10 total points wins.

ROOK

This game was originally played with a special deck designed for those who had religious objections to ordinary cards. If you're new to trick-taking games, please see the brief overview on page 11.

OBJECTIVE: Be the first team to reach 300 points.

MATERIALS: One standard 52-card deck with one Joker, a method for recording scores and bids

CARD RANKING: Natural, Aces high; with trump suit

Setup

Remove all Fours, Threes, and Twos from the deck. Players pair up in teams of two. Teammates sit opposite each other.

Dealing

Deal nine cards to each player's hand and five to a facedown pile called the "nest." A player who received no counter cards (Joker, Aces, Tens, or Fives) can call for a redeal.

Bidding

After looking at their dealt cards, players bid to gain an advantage in the hand. Bids can range from 70 to 120 and must be divisible by five. In turn, each player makes an initial bid, raises on a previous bid, or passes. If the first three players pass, the dealer automatically bids 70 and wins the bid. Otherwise, bidding continues around the table until someone bids 120 or three players pass. Players cannot bid after passing.

The winner of the bid looks at the nest and swaps up to five of its cards for the same number of cards from their hand. They also choose the trump suit for the hand. Their team must earn their bid amount in points or pay a penalty.

Playing the Game

The winner of the bid leads the first trick. Everyone else plays to the trick in turn and must follow suit if possible. If a player cannot follow suit, they may play any card from their hand. Whoever played the highest-ranking card of the led suit takes the trick unless one or more trump suit cards were played, in which case the highest-ranking trump card wins the trick. The player who takes a trick leads the next trick of the hand.

The Joker may be played on any trick regardless of the other cards a player holds. Otherwise, it is treated as the highest-ranking trump card. If the Joker is led, the led suit is the trump suit. If the trump suit is led and the player holding the Joker has no other trump cards, they must play the Joker.

When everyone is out of cards, the player who took the last trick also captures the nest. Then, each team tallies their score for the hand based on the counter cards they captured:

+ **20 points** for the Joker

+ **10 points** per Ace or Ten

+ **5 points** per Five

The team that didn't win the bid adds their score for the hand to their total score for the game. The bid-winning team does the same *if* they met or exceeded their bid. Otherwise, they earn zero points for the hand and *subtract* their bid amount from their total score. (Negative scores are possible.) When one or both teams reach a total score of 300, the team with the higher score wins.

CONTINUED

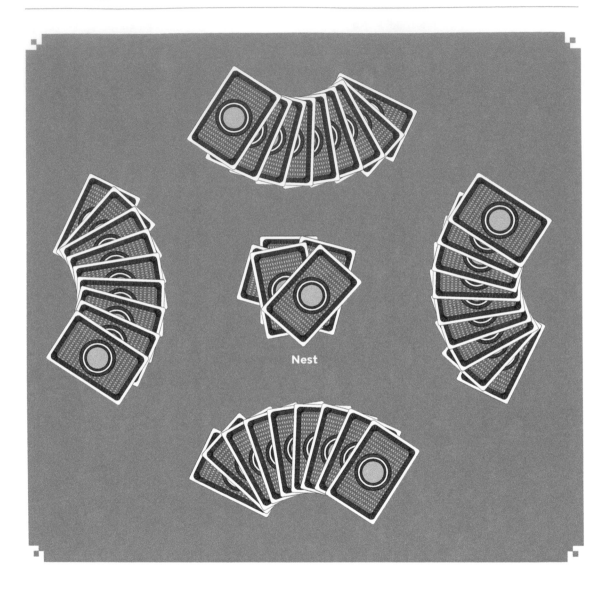

Nest

PITCH

Also called High Low Jack, Pitch has quick hands and a unique scoring system. If you're new to trick-taking games, please see the brief overview on page 11.

OBJECTIVE: Be the first player to reach 11 points.

MATERIALS: One standard 52-card deck (no Jokers), a method for recording scores and bids

CARD RANKING: Natural, Aces high; with trump suit

Dealing

Deal six cards to each player's hand, distributing them in batches of three at a time.

Terminology

Pitch uses two types of points, "pip points" and "pointy points." Don't get these mixed up! ("Pointy points" are also called "scoring points," but, well, that's just not as fun.)

Playing the Game

After looking at their hands, players bid to choose the trump suit for the hand. Bids can range from 1 to 4. Beginning with the starting player, each player makes an initial bid, raises on a previous bid, or passes. This continues until someone bids 4 or all but one player have passed. (Players cannot bid after passing.) If none of the nondealing players bids, the dealer automatically bids 2 and wins the bid. The winner of the bid is called the "pitcher"; they must earn their bid amount in pointy points during the hand or pay a penalty.

A hand is played in a series of six tricks. The pitcher leads the first trick. The suit of the first card they play is the trump suit. Everyone else plays to the trick in turn. If a player is able to follow suit, they must do so *or* play a trump card. If they can't follow suit, they may play any card from their hand. Whoever played the highest-ranking card of the led suit takes the trick unless one or more cards of the trump suit were played, in which case the highest-ranking trump card wins the trick. The player who takes a trick leads the next trick of the hand.

CONTINUED

When all six tricks have been played, four pointy points are awarded as follows:

+ The **high point** for taking the highest-ranking trump card of the hand

+ The **low point** for taking the lowest-ranking trump card of the hand

+ The **Jack point** for taking the Jack of the trump suit

+ The **game point** for taking the most pip points in tricks

Because not all cards are in play at one time, the Jack point might not be awarded. In rare cases, the high and low trump cards might be the same card. Pip points are scored based on the cards each player took in tricks (if there's a tie, nobody wins the game point):

Card Rank	Ace	King	Queen	Jack	Ten	All Others
Pip Point Value	4	3	2	1	10	0

To prevent ties, pointy points are scored *in the order listed*. The first player to score their 11th pointy point wins immediately. However, if the pitcher fails to meet or exceed their bid, they earn zero pointy points (how sad), and their bid amount is *subtracted* from their total score.

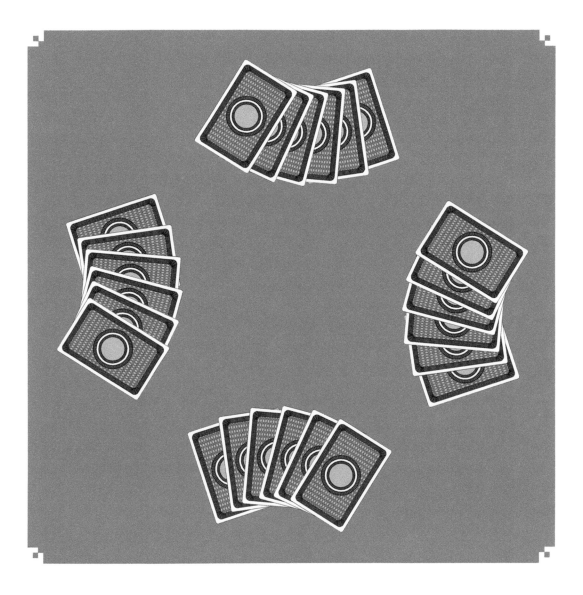

SPADES

Similar to Hearts in game play and name, Spades has the added challenge of trying to predict how many tricks you'll take in a hand. If you're new to trick-taking games, please see the brief overview on page 11.

OBJECTIVE: Be the first player or team to reach 500 points.

MATERIALS: One standard 52-card deck (no Jokers), a method for recording scores and bids

CARD RANKING: Natural, Aces high; Spades trump other suits

Setup

Players may play solo or in teams of two. Teammates sit opposite each other.

Dealing

Deal 13 cards to each player's hand.

Bidding

After looking at their dealt cards, each player in turn makes a bid from nil (zero) to 13, indicating how many tricks they think they'll take during the hand. If playing in teams, teammate bids are combined into one team bid *unless* one or both partners bids nil; a player who bids nil aims to take zero tricks while their partner tries to meet their own bid. A "blind nil" (worth double the points of a nil) is a nil bid made before the bidding player looks at their hand.

Playing the Game

A hand is played in a series of 13 tricks. The starting player leads the first trick. Everyone else plays to the trick in turn and must follow suit if possible. If they can't, they may play any card from their hand. Whoever played the highest-ranking card of the led suit takes the trick unless one or more Spades were played, in which case the highest-ranking Spade wins the trick. The player who takes a trick leads the next trick of the hand.

Unless a player has only Spade cards, Spades may not be played as the lead suit of a trick until a Spade has been played on a previous trick in the current hand. Spades may not be played during the first trick of a hand unless a player was dealt all 13 Spades. (If this ever happens to you, you might want to consider picking up a lottery ticket.)

At the end of each hand, points are awarded for meeting bids and for "bags" (tricks taken over and above one's bid amount). In a team game, if a player fails to meet a nil or blind nil bid, the tricks they take *do not* count toward their partner's bid but *do* count as bags for the team. Total bags taken are tallied alongside total score. When a player or team reaches 10 total bags, they receive –100 points as penalty and their bag count resets.

Award points for bids and bags as follows:

Bid Amount/ Type	Tricks Taken	Points Awarded
1 to 13	Less than bid amount	Multiply bid amount by –10
	Bid amount or greater	Multiply bid amount by 10, then add one point per bag
Nil	Zero	100
	One or more	–100
Blind Nil	Zero	200
	One or more	–200

Negative total scores are possible. The first player or team to reach 500 total points wins.

Variations

♦ **Short Game:** Play to 200 or 250 points.

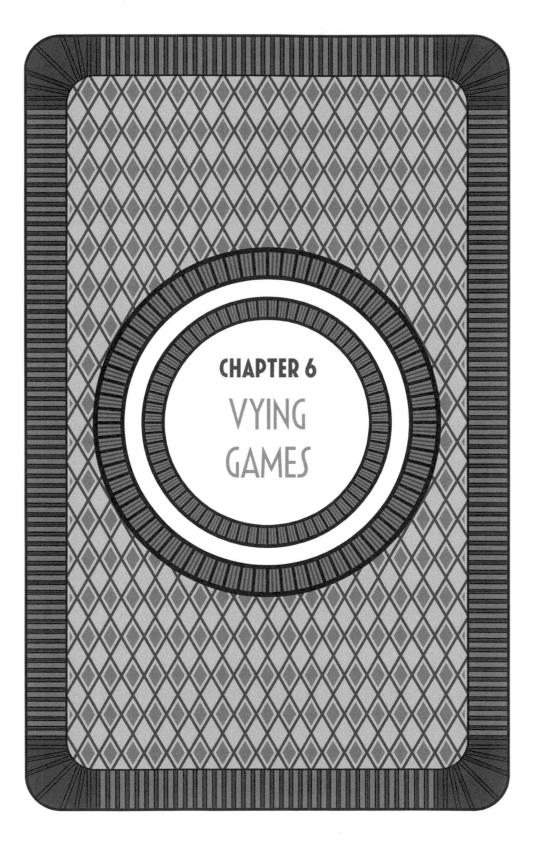

CHAPTER 6

VYING
GAMES

POKER BASICS

Poker is a large family of games with a core set of common rules. Though not every vying game is a poker game, almost all of them use poker-like language and concepts. Every game in this chapter uses terms and rules referenced here, so we highly recommend reading this overview before continuing. Though far from exhaustive, it will allow you to play the following games at a basic level.

TERMINOLOGY

Here are a dozen terms all poker players should know:

Ante: A small, mandatory bet paid by all players before a deal.

Bet: To wager one's chips in a betting round.

Blinds: Small, mandatory bets (the "small blind" and "big blind," respectively) paid at the start of each hand by the first two players after the dealer. Because the positions that pay them are relative to the dealer, the blinds are paid by different players each hand. Blinds are typically used in lieu of an ante, although it's possible to have both. Two games in this book (Texas Hold'em and Omaha Hold'em) use blinds instead of antes.

Bluff: To play deceptively, attempting to fool players with better hands into folding.

Call: To match a previous bet.

Check: To pass on making a bet without being required to fold.

Chips: Tokens that represent real or fake money.

Fold: To discard one's cards and stop participating in a hand, forfeiting chips already paid to the pot.

Hole Card: A hand card that is kept facedown on the table when not being looked at.

Kickers: Cards in a hand that don't contribute to its rank. For example, if your hand contains three Fours, a Seven, and a Jack, you have three of a kind of Fours. The Seven and Jack are the kickers; they are part of your hand but not part of the combination that gives the hand its rank (three of a kind). (Note that not all hands have kickers; some, like a full house or straight, use all five cards in the combination.)

Pot: The chips at stake during a hand, usually kept in a central pile on the table.

Raise: To bet more than a previous bet.

BETTING

The objective of poker is to take chips from other players by winning the pot into which players place their bets. Ensure that every player starts with a sufficient number of chips. To avoid confusion, players should clearly state their intended action when moving chips.

A hand of poker involves one or more rounds of betting. Bet chips are placed into the pot immediately. A designated player starts a betting round by making a bet or (if allowed) checking. If they check, the next player has the option to make a bet. If all players check, the betting round ends with no chips added to the pot. However, if a bet is made, every other player must call, raise, or fold in turn. After a raise, players must call the raised amount, raise again, or fold. If a player has already contributed chips to the pot during the same betting round, they must pay the difference when calling a raised bet. A betting round ends when every player has called or folded.

BETTING LIMITS

On a wellness note, we *strongly* recommend adhering to a reasonable, overall limit when playing any game for real money. As for actual game rules, several systems for constraining bets and raises are used in poker. Our rules use two different types:

- **Fixed-limit**, which uses "small bet" (5 to 10 times the ante or double the small blind) and "big bet" (double the small bet) amounts. A betting round will typically use *either* the small bet *or* big bet amount. Raise amounts must equal the first bet made in a round.

- **Spread-limit**, which places minimum and maximum limits (similar to the amounts in fixed-limit) on a range of bet and raise amounts.

The bet may be raised up to three times in a single betting round.

WINNING

If all players fold except one, the remaining player wins the hand uncontested and isn't required to show their hand. If multiple players complete the final betting round, a "showdown" occurs. Starting with the last player to make an "aggressive" betting action (an action that forces other players to pay chips to the pot if they don't want to fold; i.e., betting or raising), each player reveals their hand. The player with the highest-ranking hand wins the pot.

HAND RANKS

Hands are ranked according to card combinations they contain. To break a tie, compare the ranks of cards within the combination (first the highest card, then the second-highest, etc.). The player whose cards are higher wins. If the cards in the combination are exactly matched, compare the ranks of the kickers (if there are any) the same way. Card ranks are natural with Aces high. If the tie isn't breakable, the winners split the pot.

Hand Name/Combination	Notes
Royal Flush (Ace, King, Queen, Jack, and Ten of one suit)	
Straight Flush (five-card run, all one suit)	
Four of a Kind	
Full House (three of a kind plus a pair)	Higher three-card set wins a tie.
Flush (five cards of one suit)	
Straight (five-card run, mixed suits)	
Three of a Kind	
Two Pair	To break a tie, compare the higher pair, then the lower pair, then the kicker.
Pair	
High Card	A high-card "combination" is simply the highest card in the hand. The other four cards are all kickers. This hand wins by beating other high-card hands in a tiebreaker.

THREE-CARD BRAG

A descendent of Primero (page 173) and an ancestor of poker, Three-Card Brag has a betting system that is a game of chicken. Though not itself a poker game, it uses similar terms and betting rules. Please see page 156 for an overview of poker basics before continuing.

OBJECTIVE: Win chips from opposing players.

MATERIALS: One standard 52-card deck (no Jokers), betting chips

CARD RANKING: Natural, Aces high except in runs

BETTING TYPE: Spread-limit

Setup

Distribute an equal number of betting chips to each player. Establish ante, minimum, and maximum bet amounts.

Dealing

After everyone has paid their ante to the pot, deal three cards to each player's hand. Traditionally, after the first hand, the dealer only shuffles the deck if a player showed their hand and won the pot with a prial (three of a kind) in the previous hand. Otherwise, the cards used in the previous hand are placed on the bottom of the deck and the next hand is immediately dealt from the top.

Playing the Game

Each player in turn must make an opening bet or fold. After the opening bet, each player that follows must match the previous bet, raise, or fold. Regardless of chips already contributed to the pot, each player must pay the *full* amount of the previous bet on every turn if they don't wish to fold. There is no limit to the number of times the bet may be raised.

The betting cycle ends in one of two ways:

♦ All but one player folds, in which case the remaining player automatically wins the pot (their cards need not be shown).

♦ Two players remain and one pays double the bet amount for a "see" (the opportunity to see the other player's hand, and vice versa). Whoever has the higher-ranked hand wins the pot.

Hand Rankings

If both players have hands of the same rank, the winner is the one whose combination uses higher-ranked cards. If these cards rank the same, the winner is the hand with higher-ranked kickers, if any. If both hands are equal in every respect, the winner is the player who *didn't* pay for the see.

Hand Rankings (Highest to Lowest)		
Hand Name	**Combination**	**Notes**
Prial	Three of a kind	
Running Flush	A three-card run of one suit	In a Run or Running Flush, an Ace can rank high *or* low. Oddly enough, a run of Ace, King, and Queen is the *second-highest* run; a run of Ace, Two, and Three outranks it.
Run	A three-card run of mixed suits	
Flush	Any three cards of the same suit	
Pair	Two of a kind	
High Card	The highest card in a hand containing none of the above combinations	Wins by beating other high-card hands in a tiebreaker.

FIVE-CARD STUD

2 TO 10 PLAYERS   **MEDIUM** | **LENGTH OF PLAY:** 2 TO 5 MINUTES PER HAND

The original stud poker, Five-Card Stud, originated during the American Civil War. See page 156 for an overview of poker basics and page 164 for a popular variant, Seven-Card Stud.

OBJECTIVE: Win chips from opposing players.

MATERIALS: One standard 52-card deck (no Jokers), betting chips

BETTING TYPE: Fixed-limit

Setup

Establish ante, small bet, and big bet amounts.

Playing the Game

A hand involves four betting rounds known as "Second Street" through "Fifth Street." In the Second Street and Third Street rounds, bet and raise amounts must equal the small bet. In Fourth Street and Fifth Street, they must equal the big bet. Checking is permitted in all rounds.

When everyone has paid the ante, the dealer deals one hole card and one faceup card to each player. The player with the lowest-ranking upcard starts the Second Street betting round; all others are started by the player whose upcards form the highest-ranking poker hand (considering sets and high cards only). Before the Third Street, Fourth Street, and Fifth Street rounds, each player who hasn't folded receives another faceup card from the dealer.

The Showdown

Each player turns up their hole card and shows their complete hand.

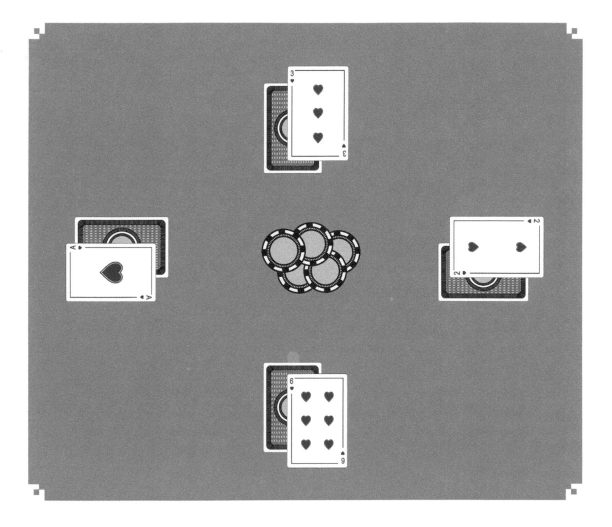

SEVEN-CARD STUD

2 TO 7 PLAYERS **MEDIUM** | **LENGTH OF PLAY:** 2 TO 5 MINUTES PER HAND

Before Texas Hold'em (page 176) exploded in popularity, this was America's favorite poker game. Please see page 156 for an overview of poker basics before continuing.

OBJECTIVE: Win chips from opposing players.

MATERIALS: One standard 52-card deck (no Jokers), betting chips

BETTING TYPE: Fixed-limit

Setup

Establish ante, small bet, and big bet amounts.

Playing the Game

A hand involves five betting rounds known as "Third Street" through "Seventh Street." In the Third Street and Fourth Street rounds, bet and raise amounts must equal the small bet. In the rest, they must equal the big bet. Checking is permitted in all rounds.

When everyone has paid the ante, the dealer deals two hole cards and one faceup card to each player. The player with the lowest-ranking upcard starts the Third Street betting round. From Fourth Street onward, the betting rounds are started by the player whose upcards form the highest-ranking poker hand (considering sets and high cards only). Before the Fourth Street, Fifth Street, and Sixth Street rounds, each player who hasn't folded receives another faceup card from the dealer. Before the Seventh Street round, they receive a facedown card.

The Showdown

Each player turns up their downcards and discards any two of their seven cards. What remains is their final hand.

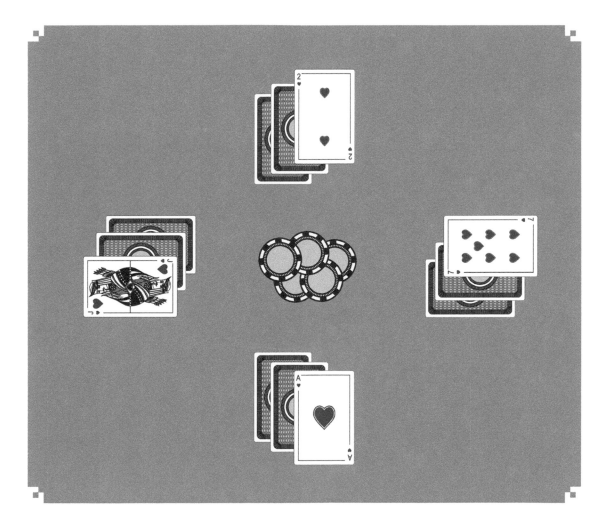

FOLLOW THE QUEEN

2 TO 7 PLAYERS   **MEDIUM** | **LENGTH OF PLAY:** 2 TO 5 MINUTES PER HAND

Not only does Follow the Queen introduce wild cards to Seven-Card Stud, the rank assigned as wild can change during a hand. Please see page 156 for an overview of poker basics before continuing.

OBJECTIVE: Win chips from opposing players.

MATERIALS: One standard 52-card deck (no Jokers), betting chips

BETTING TYPE: Fixed-limit

Playing the Game

Follow the Queen is played exactly like Seven-Card Stud (page 164) with one major difference: any time a Queen is dealt faceup, the *next* card to be dealt faceup becomes wild, as do all other cards of the same rank. If another Queen is turned up in the same hand, the previous wild cards are no longer wild, and the next faceup card (along with all cards of matching rank) becomes wild. If a Queen is turned up as the final faceup card of a hand, it cancels any previous wilds, and there are no wild cards going into the showdown.

Ranking Hands with Wild Cards

With wild cards in play, the otherwise-unseen "five of a kind" rank becomes possible. If acquired, this hand outranks all others. If ties between equally ranked hands need to be broken, wild cards are counted as the rank of the card they replace.

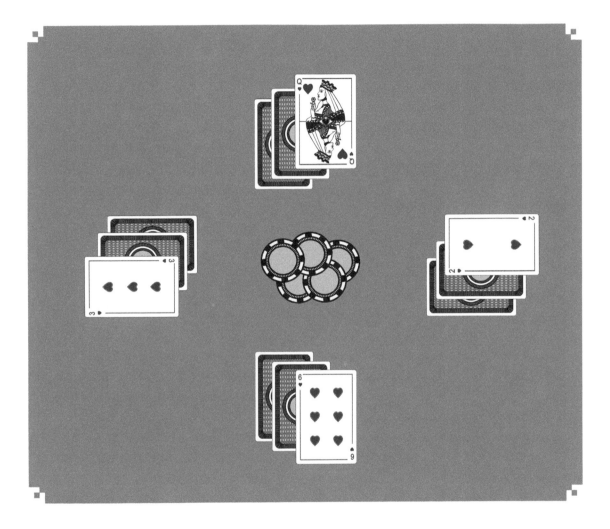

FOUR OF A KIND

Though not a poker game, Four of a Kind uses similar terms and betting rules. Please see page 156 for an overview of poker basics before continuing.

OBJECTIVE: Win chips from opposing players.

MATERIALS: One standard 52-card deck (no Jokers)

CARD RANKING: Natural, Aces high

BETTING TYPE: Spread-limit

Setup

Establish ante, minimum, and maximum bet amounts.

Playing the Game

When everyone has paid the ante, the dealer deals one card faceup to each player. If any card matches the rank of a previous card, it is shuffled back into the stock and a new card is dealt to replace it. When all players have cards of different ranks, the player with the highest-ranking card starts a betting round. Checking is permitted.

After the betting round, the dealer begins turning up stock cards one at a time. When a turned-up card matches the rank of any player's card, it is dealt to that player if they haven't folded. Dealing pauses and another betting round is started by the player with the most cards (if tied, the player with *higher-ranking* cards starts). Checking is permitted. After the betting round, dealing resumes. This process repeats until a player is holding four of a kind. This player wins half the pot. The player with the fewest cards wins the other half (if tied, the player with *lower-ranking* cards wins).

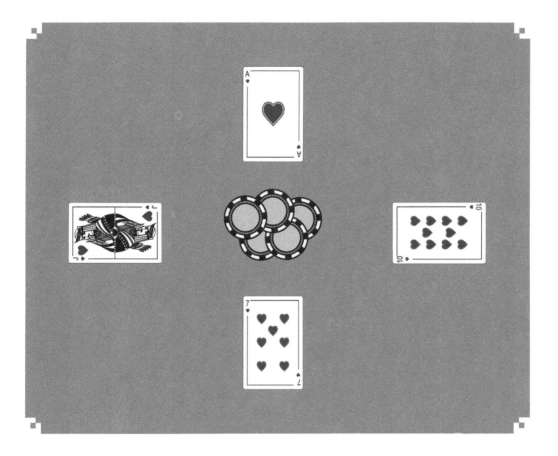

BOUILLOTTE

This 18th-century French game uses poker-style terms and betting rules. Please see page 156 for an overview of poker basics before continuing.

OBJECTIVE: Win chips from opposing players.

MATERIALS: One standard 52-card deck (no Jokers), betting chips

NUMERICAL CARD VALUES: Ace = 11, face card = 10, number card = rank value

BETTING TYPE: Spread-limit

Setup

Use Aces, Kings, Queens, Nines, and Eights only. Establish ante, minimum, and maximum bet amounts.

Playing the Game

When the ante is paid, the dealer pays double. The starting player begins a betting round with checking permitted. Following this, the dealer deals a three-card hand to *every* player (including any who folded) and one shared, faceup card (the "*retourné*"). The last player to bet or raise (or, if everyone checked, the starting player) starts a second betting round.

The Showdown

Hand ranks in descending order are *brélan carré* (four of a kind), *simple brélan* (three of a kind in hand), and *brélan favori* (three of a kind including the *retourné*). All players, including any who folded, give one chip to anyone with a ranked hand plus one more for a *brélan carré*.

Only players who haven't folded can win the pot. If nobody has a ranked hand, sum up the numerical values of all hand cards of each suit. Whoever holds the highest-ranking card of the highest-valued suit wins the pot.

SEVEN TWENTY-SEVEN

4 TO 10 PLAYERS | **MEDIUM** | **LENGTH OF PLAY:** 5 TO 10 MINUTES PER HAND

Which pot do you want? This game doesn't make you choose. Seven Twenty-Seven is not a poker game but uses similar terms and betting rules. Please see page 156 for an overview of poker basics before continuing.

OBJECTIVE: Win chips from opposing players.

MATERIALS: One standard 52-card deck (no Jokers)

NUMERICAL CARD VALUES: Ace = 1 and 11, face card = 0.5, number card = rank value

BETTING TYPE: Spread-limit

Setup

Establish ante, minimum, and maximum bet amounts.

Playing the Game

When everyone has paid the ante, the dealer deals one hole card and one upcard to each player. One or more betting rounds follow. After each betting round, remaining players decide whether they will receive another downcard from the dealer. If nobody receives a new card, the game moves to a showdown. Otherwise, another betting round begins.

Betting rounds are started by the first player in turn order who hasn't folded. Checking is permitted.

The Showdown

Each player whose total hand value is closest to 7 or 27 wins half the pot. If multiple players are equally close to one of the target values, the corresponding half of the pot is split between them. Aces are worth 1 when counting toward 7 and 11 when counting toward 27, allowing a player to aim for (and possibly win) both sides of the pot at once.

CONTINUED

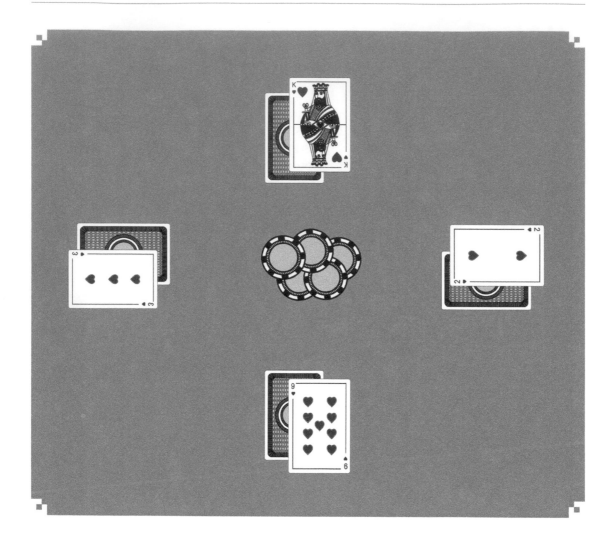

PRIMERO

Primero dates back to the Renaissance and was popular enough to be mentioned by Shakespeare. Though versions of it are reportedly still played in parts of the world, no concrete record of the original rules is known to exist. The following rules were derived from a variety of sources, including reconstructions based on descriptions found in European literature. Though not a form of poker, Primero uses similar terms and betting rules. Please see page 156 for an overview of poker basics before continuing.

OBJECTIVE: Win chips from opposing players.

MATERIALS: One standard 52-card deck (no Jokers), betting chips

NUMERICAL CARD VALUES: Seven = 21, Six = 18, Ace = 16, Five = 15, Four = 14, Three = 13, Two = 12, face card = 10

Setup

Remove all Tens, Nines, and Eights from the deck. Establish ante and minimum bet amounts.

Betting Round Rules

The dealer (or the first player still in the game, if the dealer has folded) starts each betting round. Checking is always allowed. There is no maximum bet amount. However, a bet or raise does not take effect unless one other player agrees to accept it. If all other players reject a bet or raise, it is withdrawn, and the betting turn passes to the next player. If one player accepts it, then it takes effect as normal.

Playing the Game

When everyone has paid the ante, the dealer deals two cards to each player's hand. The first betting round takes place. The dealer deals two more cards to every player who hasn't folded. Another betting round takes place. Finally, the dealer deals eight cards facedown in the middle of the table, forming a grid of two rows by four columns.

CONTINUED

Starting with the dealer (or the first player who hasn't folded), each player in turn draws a card from the table and replaces it with one from their hand. When the last player before the dealer has taken their turn, a betting round takes place. This happens every time the turns make a full cycle around the table. If, at any point, all players have folded except one, the remaining player wins uncontested. Otherwise, when a player is satisfied with their hand, they knock on the table *on their next turn* and make no further swaps. When a second player knocks, play immediately stops and the game moves to a showdown.

The Showdown

The player with the highest-ranking hand wins the pot. If there's a tie for highest hand rank, the numerical values of the cards *in the combinations* (not including kickers) are added together. The player whose combination has the highest total value wins the pot. If there are no ranked hands, the pot goes to the player whose cards add up to the highest numerical value.

Hand Rankings (Highest to Lowest)	
Name	**Combination**
Chorus	Four of a kind
Fluxus	Four-card flush
Punto	Ace, Seven, Six, and Jack (suits irrelevant)
Supremus	Ace, Seven, and Six of one suit
Primero	One card of each suit
Numerus	Any two or three cards of one suit

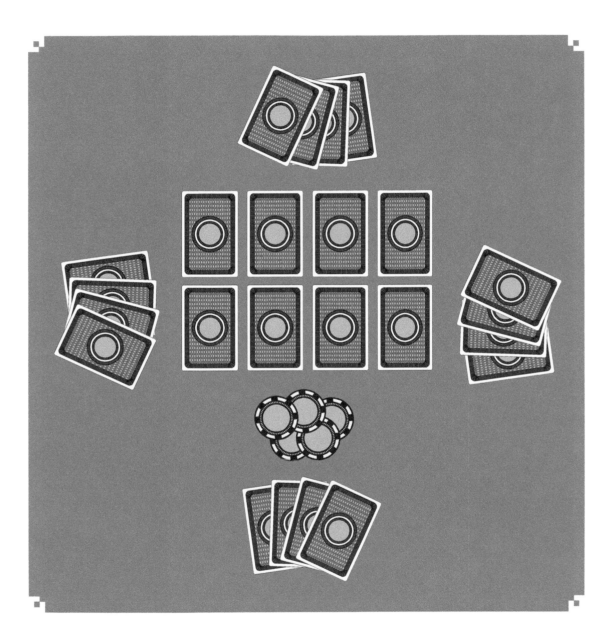

TEXAS HOLD'EM

2+ PLAYERS   **HARD** | **LENGTH OF PLAY:** 2 TO 10 MINUTES PER HAND

This game's popularity exploded in the early 2000s thanks to televised tournaments and extensive media exposure. Please see page 156 for an overview of poker basics before continuing.

OBJECTIVE: Win chips from opposing players.

MATERIALS: One standard 52-card deck (no Jokers), betting chips

BETTING TYPE: Fixed-limit

Setup

Establish small bet, big bet, small blind (half the small bet), and big blind (equal to the small bet) amounts.

Playing the Game

The first two players pay the small blind and big blind, respectively. The dealer deals two hole cards to each player, and a betting round begins. In this first betting round, the big blind is treated as the opening bet; players must call or raise by this amount if they don't want to fold. The payer of the small blind need only pay the difference (subtracting the small blind amount they already paid) if they call or raise.

After the first betting round, the dealer deals the "flop" (three shared, faceup cards), "turn" (a fourth shared card), and "river" (a fifth shared card) onto the table. Each deal precedes a betting round that's started by the first player in turn order who hasn't folded. Checking is permitted in these rounds. After the flop, bet and raise amounts must equal the small bet. After the turn and river, they must equal the big bet.

The Showdown

Each player turns up their hole cards and forms the best possible poker hand using five of the seven cards available to them.

OMAHA HOLD'EM

2+ PLAYERS   HARD | LENGTH OF PLAY: 2 TO 10 MINUTES PER HAND

This game is a lesser-known cousin of Texas Hold'em (page 176). Please see page 156 for an overview of poker basics before continuing.

BETTING TYPE: Fixed-limit

OBJECTIVE: Win chips from opposing players.

MATERIALS: One standard 52-card deck (no Jokers), betting chips

Setup

Establish small bet, big bet, small blind (half the small bet), and big blind (equal to the small bet) amounts.

Playing the Game

The first two players pay the small blind and big blind, respectively. The dealer deals four hole cards to each player, and a betting round begins. In this first betting round, the big blind is treated as the opening bet; players must call or raise by this amount if they don't want to fold. The payer of the small blind need only pay the difference (subtracting the small blind amount they already paid) if they call or raise.

After the first betting round, the dealer deals the "flop" (three shared, faceup cards), "turn" (a fourth shared card), and "river" (a fifth shared card) onto the table. Each deal precedes a betting round that's started by the first player in turn order who hasn't folded. Checking is permitted in these rounds. After the flop, bet and raise amounts must equal the small bet. After the turn and river, they must equal the big bet.

The Showdown

Each player turns up their hole cards and forms the best possible poker hand using *two* cards from their hand and *three* of the shared cards on the table.

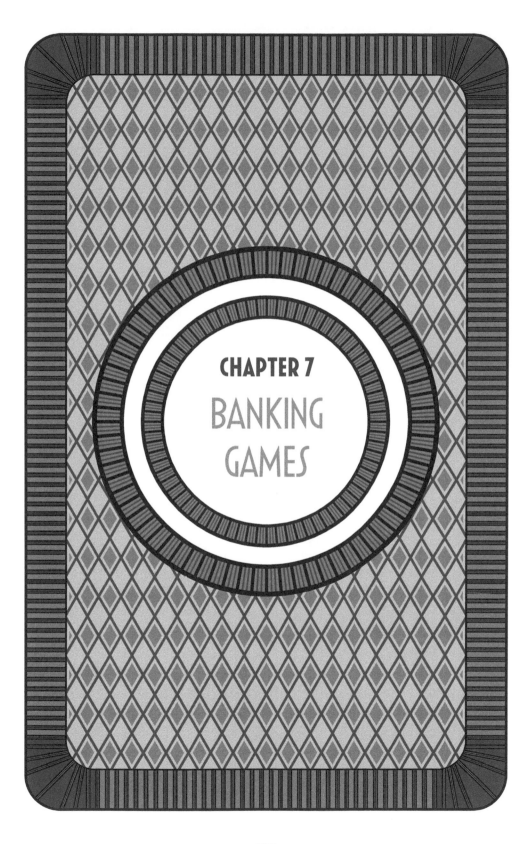

CHAPTER 7

BANKING
GAMES

BACCARAT

2+ PLAYERS   EASY | LENGTH OF PLAY: LESS THAN 1 MINUTE PER HAND

Aside from the betting, Baccarat is more-or-less automatic. If you're new to banking games, please see the brief overview on page 12.

OBJECTIVE: Win chips from opposing players.

MATERIALS: 6 to 8 standard 52-card decks (no Jokers), betting chips

NUMERICAL CARD VALUES: Ace = 1, Two to Nine = rank value, Ten to King = zero

Playing the Game

Each player bets on whether the "player's hand" or the "banker's hand" will win. Alternately, they may bet that the hands will tie. The dealer deals both hands faceup and places two cards in each. To determine the numerical value of each hand, first add together the values of the individual cards. Then, if the sum total is 10 or higher, subtract 10; for example, if the cards add up to 13, the value of the hand is 3. The final value should always be between 0 and 9. Third cards are dealt as follows:

♦ The player's hand receives another card if it's worth 5 or less *and* the banker's hand is worth 7 or less.

♦ If the player's hand *did not* receive another card, the banker's hand receives one if it's worth 5 or less.

♦ If the player's hand *did* receive another card, the banker's hand receives one if:

The player's 3rd card is worth:	0	1	2	3	4	5	6	7	8	9
and the banker's hand is worth less than:	4		5		6		7		3	4

If a hand receives a third card, its new value is calculated using the same method described above. The hand with the highest final value wins. Players win and lose bets accordingly. If the hands are tied, each player who bet on a tie wins eight times their bet; all others keep their bets.

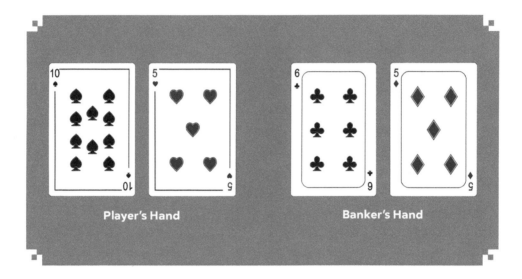

Player's Hand   Banker's Hand

FARO

In this game, the first card dealt is called "soda." In researching to discover why, we only found speculation, rumor, and a 1949 book called *Scarne on Cards* in which card expert John Scarne asked whether "some etymologist" could answer the same question for him. I don't think we'll be getting an answer anytime soon. If you're new to banking games, please see the brief overview on page 12.

OBJECTIVE: Win chips from opposing players.

MATERIALS: Two standard 52-card decks (no Jokers), betting chips, one "copper" (a penny or some other token distinct from the betting chips) per player

Setup

From one deck, take 13 cards of the same suit and arrange them in an orderly table layout, faceup and in natural rank order (Ace low). (Traditionally, and likely as a space-saving measure, the cards are arranged in a row that curves back on itself like a narrow horseshoe. The Ace and King, on the ends of the row, end up close to one another. The Seven is on the apex of the curve.) Place the remainder of the first deck aside; the banker will deal from the second (full) deck.

Playing the Game

The banker deals one card, called "soda," faceup. Following this, each player places bets on one or more layout cards. Placing a "copper" on top of the chips means the player wins the bet if the card loses. The banker deals two cards, one to the right of soda and the second on top of soda. A layout card that matches the first card's rank loses; one that matches the second card wins. If both cards have the same rank, the banker takes half of any bet placed on that rank.

The banker continues dealing cards in twos as described. Between deals, players may retract and add bets. Before the final deal, a player may place a side bet on the order in which the final three cards will be dealt. For a correct guess, they win quadruple the bet (reduced to double if the final cards contain a pair).

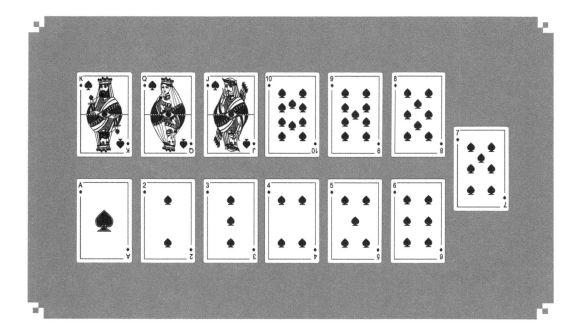

IN BETWEEN

Also called Acey Deucey, Yablon, and Red Dog, this one has a surprising number of names for such a simple game. If you're new to banking games, please see the brief overview on page 12.

OBJECTIVE: Win chips from opposing players.

MATERIALS: One standard 52-card deck (no Jokers), betting chips

CARD RANKING: Natural, Aces high

Playing the Game

All nonbanking players bet on winning the hand. The banker deals two cards faceup. If the two cards are adjacent in rank, the hand is a "push" (draw) and all players keep their bets. If the two cards are the same rank, the banker immediately deals a third card. If it's the same rank as the first two, all players win 11 times their bet amount; otherwise, they keep their bets.

In all other cases, players have the option to increase their bet by an amount no larger than their original bet. Then, the banker deals a third card. If the third card's rank falls between the ranks of the first two, all players win their bets. Otherwise, they lose. The amount a player wins may be multiplied depending on the "spread" (the number of ranks between the first two cards). If the spread is 1, players win five times their bet; if it's 2, they win four times their bet; if it's 3, they win double their bet.

ANDAR BAHAR

2+ PLAYERS   **EASY** | **LENGTH OF PLAY:** LESS THAN 1 MINUTE PER HAND

In Hindi, *Andar* means "inside" and *Bahar* means "outside." If you're new to banking games, please see the brief overview on page 12.

OBJECTIVE: Win chips from opposing players.

MATERIALS: One standard 52-card deck (no Jokers), betting chips

Playing the Game

On the table are two spaces called Andar and Bahar. The banker deals one faceup card directly between these two spaces. This card goes by a variety of names; for simplicity, we'll call it the "middle card." Each player bets on either Andar or Bahar. Then, the banker begins rapidly dealing cards onto the two spaces, alternating between them with each new card. If the middle card is black, the first card is dealt to Andar; if it's red, the first card goes to Bahar. When a card is dealt that matches the rank of the middle card, the dealing stops. Players who bet on the space that received the matching card win their bets; all others lose.

SEVEN AND A HALF

In Italy, this game is traditionally played around Christmas. If you're new to banking games, please see the brief overview on page 12.

MATERIALS: One standard 52-card deck (no Jokers), betting chips

OBJECTIVE: Win chips from opposing players.

NUMERICAL CARD VALUES: Ace = 1, face card = 0.5, number card = rank value

Setup

Remove all Eights, Nines, and Tens from the deck.

Game Structure

Each player has a "count" worth the total numerical value of all of their cards. If a count exceeds 7.5, it's a "bust." A player wins by having a higher count than the banker without busting. In the case of a tie, the banker wins.

Playing the Game

Each nonbanking player places a bet on winning the hand. The banker deals one face-down card to each player, including themselves. After looking at their card, each player in turn decides whether they will "stay" (end their turn with their current cards) or request additional cards from the banker. Additional cards are dealt faceup and requested one at a time until the player busts or chooses to stay. If their count reaches exactly 7.5, they must immediately reveal their downcard.

When all players have taken their turns, the banker turns up their downcard and plays their own hand. If the banker busts, all nonbusted players automatically win.

BLACKJACK

2+ PLAYERS   **MEDIUM** | **LENGTH OF PLAY:** LESS THAN 1 MINUTE PER HAND

A banking game of the Twenty-One family, Blackjack is one of the most recognizable card games in the world. If you're new to banking games, please see the brief overview on page 12.

OBJECTIVE: Win chips from opposing players.

MATERIALS: One standard 52-card deck (no Jokers), betting chips

NUMERICAL CARD VALUES: Ace = 1 or 11, face card = 10, number card = rank value

Game Structure

Each player has a "count" worth the total numerical value of all of their cards. If a player's count exceeds 21, it's a "bust" and results in an immediate loss. A player wins by having a higher count than the banker without busting. In the case of a "push" (tie), the player keeps their bet.

Playing the Game

Before a deal, each nonbanking player places a bet on winning the hand. The banker deals one faceup card to each player and one to themselves. This is repeated once with the banker's second card dealt facedown. The banker does not look at their downcard unless their upcard is an Ace, Ten, or face card.

If the upcard is one of these cards, it's possible that the banker has a "blackjack" (an ace paired with a Ten or face card for a total count of 21). If the upcard is an Ace, players have the option to "buy insurance" (place a side bet worth half their original bet) against the banker having a blackjack before the banker checks their downcard.

If the banker has a blackjack, the hand is a push for any player who also has a blackjack and a loss for any player who does not; any player who "bought insurance" wins twice their insurance bet. If the banker does not have a blackjack, all insurance bets are lost and any player who has a blackjack immediately wins. The hand continues as normal for all other players.

All of a player's remaining actions are performed in a single turn. When the banker faces them, they may do any of the following:

- **Stand:** End their turn with their current cards.

- **Hit:** Request another card (dealt faceup) from the banker. This may be done repeatedly until the player busts or chooses to stand.

- **Double Down:** Double their bet and receive one more card.

- **Split:** If the player was dealt a pair, they may double their bet and separate the two cards. The banker deals one card beside each of the original cards to create two individual hands, which the player plays one at a time. Half of the doubled bet is wagered on each hand.

When all players have taken their turns, the banker turns up their downcard and plays their own hand. They must hit until they reach a total of 17 or higher, at which point they stand. If the banker busts, all nonbusted players automatically win.

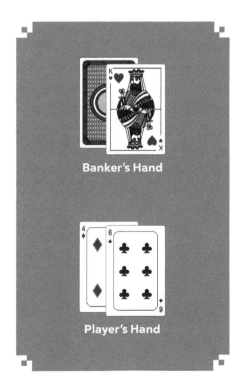

SKIN

Skin may not be a "true" banking game, because nonbanking players can compete with each other. It is truly unique, however. If you're new to banking games, please see the brief overview on page 12.

OBJECTIVE: Win chips from opposing players.

MATERIALS: One standard 52-card deck (no Jokers), betting chips

Playing the Game

The banker draws cards one at a time throughout the hand. (For now, we're going to assume that every card drawn is a different rank. We'll address what happens with matches later on.) The first card drawn is given to the starting player, who takes the first turn. A player's turn involves deciding whether to accept or reject a card given to them. If they reject it, they pass it to the next player who doesn't already have a card. This player has the same choice to accept or reject the card. If all nonbanking players reject a card, it is placed faceup in the middle of the table. On a turn when they would normally receive a card from the banker, a player may choose to take a card from the middle instead.

When a player accepts a card handed to them or takes one from the middle, they place it in front of them and make a bet that the banker's card will be matched before their own. If the banker does not already have a card, they must take the next card from the stock or one from the middle of the table. The player then states a maximum amount they wish to bet. The banker places a bet no higher than this maximum on the player's card, which the player must match.

Players may not have multiple cards at once. When the banker draws a new card to hand to a player, it is given to the next player in turn order (after the most recent player to accept or reject a card) who doesn't already have a card. If all players have cards, drawn cards are placed straight into the middle.

When the banker draws a card that matches the rank of a card already drawn, both are discarded, and the rank is considered "dead." If a dead card on the table belongs to a nonbanking player, the banker wins their bet against that player and takes any chips on the card. If the dead card belongs to the banker, the banker loses *all* active bets; all players win the chips on their own cards. If a dead card is drawn, it is discarded.

If the banker loses their card, they may take one of the middle cards *or* the next unmatched card that is drawn. They are not required to do either unless a player receives a new card and places a bet against them.

In addition to bets against the banker, players with cards in play may place "side bets" against one another. Two players bet an agreed-upon amount, and one player wins the combined chips when the other's card is matched. The hand is over when all banker and side bets are resolved.

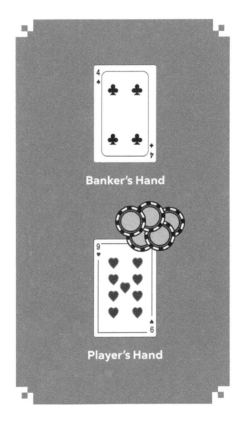

THREE-CARD POKER

Invented in 1994, this vague approximation of poker is a recent addition to casino table games. If you're new to banking games, please see the brief overview on page 12.

OBJECTIVE: Win chips from opposing players.

MATERIALS: One standard 52-card deck (no Jokers), betting chips

CARD RANKING: Natural, Aces high except in runs

Playing the Game

Nonbanking players must place one or both of the following bets in designated spots on the table:

- ♦ **Ante:** A bet that allows a player to play their hand against the banker's. Must be followed up by a "play" bet after the deal for the player to keep playing.

- ♦ **Pair plus:** A bet placed on the chances of a player's hand containing a pair or better. The value of the banker's hand is irrelevant to winning this bet.

When all bets are placed, the banker deals three cards to each player's hand. Players who placed an ante must now place a "play" bet equal to the ante if they wish to follow through on playing against the banker. Otherwise, they must "fold," forfeiting the ante.

The banker reveals their hand, which must be a "Queen high" (a high-card hand in which the highest card is a Queen) or higher for them to be eligible to play. If the banker isn't eligible to play, all players who didn't fold win their ante bets and keep their play bets. Otherwise, the banker compares their hand against each player who made a play bet. If the player's hand beats the banker's, the player wins their ante and play bets. If the banker's hand beats the player's, the player loses both bets. If both hands have the same rank, the tie is broken by comparing the ranks of cards within the combination (first the highest card, then the second-highest, etc.) followed by the ranks of any "kickers" (cards not part of the combination). If the tie can't be broken, the player keeps both bets.

Even if they didn't beat the banker, certain hands award multiples of the ante bet as a bonus to players who didn't fold. Furthermore, a player who made a pair-plus bet wins multiples of that bet if they have a pair or better; it doesn't matter whether they played against the banker or not. These payouts and their associated hand ranks are as follows:

Hand Rankings (Highest to Lowest)				
Hand Name	Combination	Pair Plus Payout	Ante Bonus Payout	Notes
Straight Flush	A three-card run of one suit	40x	5x	Aces count high or low.
Three of a Kind	Three cards of the same rank	30x	4x	
Straight	A three-card run of mixed suits	6x	1x	Aces count high or low.
Flush	Any three cards of the same suit	4x	0x (no bonus)	
Pair	Two of a kind	1x		
High Card	The highest card in a hand containing none of the above combinations	0x (pair-plus bet lost)		Wins by beating another high-card hand in a tiebreaker.

CONTINUED

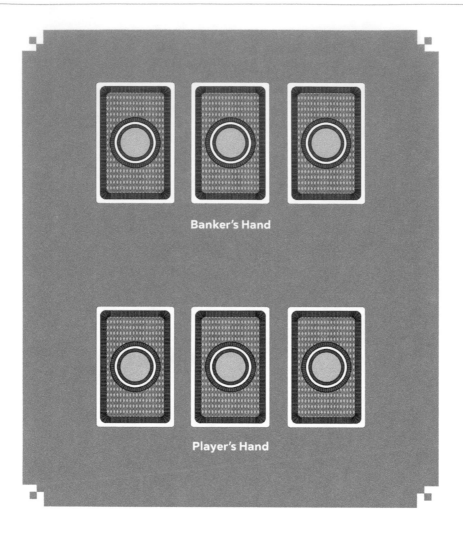

Banker's Hand

Player's Hand

PONTOON

2+ PLAYERS   **HARD** | **LENGTH OF PLAY:** 2 TO 5 MINUTES PER HAND

A cousin of Blackjack (page 190), Pontoon is a British form of Twenty-One. If you're new to banking games, please see the brief overview on page 12.

OBJECTIVE: Win chips from opposing players.

MATERIALS: One standard 52-card deck (no Jokers), betting chips

NUMERICAL CARD VALUES: Ace = 1 or 11, face card = 10, number card = rank value

Game Structure

Each player has a "count" worth the total numerical value of all of their cards. If a count exceeds 21, it's a "bust" and results in an immediate loss.

There are three ranked hand types:

+ **Pontoon:** An Ace paired with a Ten or face card

+ **Five-Card Trick:** Five cards with a count of 21 or less

+ **Twenty-One:** Three or four cards with a count of exactly 21

The first player to beat the banker with a pontoon becomes the banker in the next hand. The banker may also "sell" the banker position for chips.

Playing the Game

The banker deals one card to each player's hand. After looking at their cards, each nonbanking player places a bet on winning the hand, bearing in mind that they may wind up losing or winning *double* this amount. (If they lose double, they must pay chips in addition to the ones they've already placed on the table.) The banker deals a second card to each player. If the banker has a pontoon, the hand is over, and each player loses twice their bet amount to the banker. Otherwise, each player takes a turn performing any of the following actions:

CONTINUED

- **Stick:** End their turn with their current cards. The count must be 15 or higher. If they have a pontoon, they immediately declare and reveal it.

- **Buy:** Increase their bet and receive another card from the banker. This may be done repeatedly until the player has five cards, busts, or chooses to stick. On the first buy, the increase to their bet must fall between one and two times the original bet. On following buys, the increase must fall between the original bet and the previous increase.

- **Twist:** Like buying but without increasing the bet. A player may twist after buying but may not buy after twisting.

- **Split:** If the player was dealt a pair, they may double their bet and separate the two cards. The banker deals two more cards to create two individual hands. Half of the bet is wagered on each hand.

When all other players have taken their turns, the banker turns up their own cards and deals themselves up to three additional cards. Whether a player wins or loses their bet, and whether or not the amount is doubled, depends on how the banker's hand ranks relative to their own hand. Compare the two hands using the following chart to determine the outcome:

		Banker Hand			
		Five-Card Trick	Twenty-One	Other	Bust
Player Hand	**Pontoon**	Player wins double			
	Five-Card Trick	Banker wins double	Banker wins	Player wins double	
	Twenty-One			Player wins	Player wins
	Other			The player wins *if* their count exceeds the banker's; otherwise, the banker wins.	Player wins

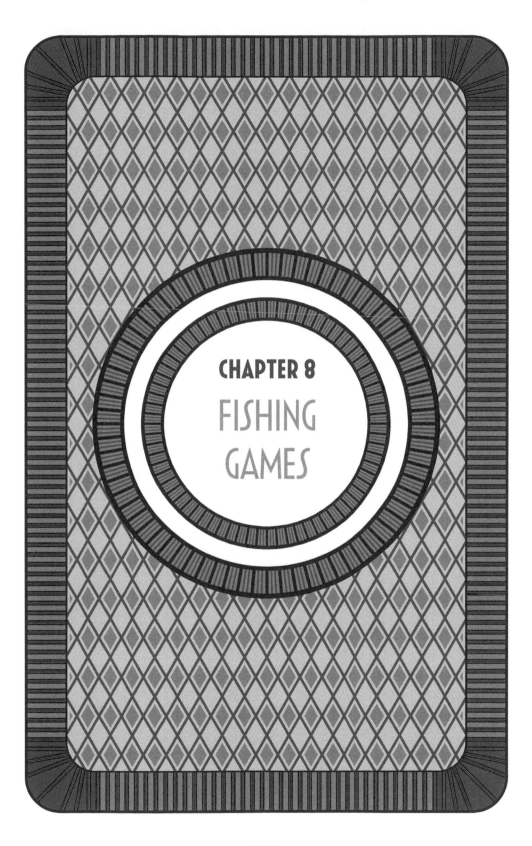

CHAPTER 8

FISHING
GAMES

MAIN MERAH

2 OR 3 PLAYERS   **EASY** | **LENGTH OF PLAY:** 5 TO 10 MINUTES

An Indonesian game similar to Chinese Ten (page 204), "Main Merah" literally means "Play Red."

OBJECTIVE: Capture the most points!

MATERIALS: One standard 52-card deck (no Jokers)

Dealing

The number of cards dealt out depends on the number of players:

Number of Players	Cards Dealt to Hands	Cards Turned Up
2	10	12
3	7	10

Deal a hand to each player, place the stock in the center of the table, and turn up the appropriate number of cards in an orderly configuration around it. If more than two Fives, Tens, Jacks, Queens, or Kings are turned up, the hand is a misdeal. If more than two of any other card are turned up, look for cards in the tableau that are the capture-counterparts of those cards; if there are five or more cards bearing these two ranks, the hand is a misdeal.

Playing the Game

Turns are played as in Chinese Ten (page 204) except that Fives, Tens, Jacks, Queens, and Kings only capture one card at a time. Players earn points for their captured cards as follows:

Card Captured	Points Awarded
Two through Eight of Hearts or Diamonds	Rank value of the captured card
Nine through King of Hearts or Diamonds	10
Ace of Hearts or Diamonds	20

The player with the highest score wins.

CHINESE TEN

This game's Chinese name means "pick up red spots."

OBJECTIVE: Capture the most points!

MATERIALS: One standard 52-card deck (no Jokers)

Dealing

Take 24 cards from the deck and deal them into equal hands for all players. Place the stock facedown in the middle of the table and turn up the top four cards around it.

Playing the Game

Each turn, a player plays one card from their hand faceup on the table. A played card will capture table cards according to the following rules:

♦ A Ten or face card captures *one* card of its own rank *unless* there are three cards of its rank on the table, in which case it must capture all three. (This prevents the possibility of uncapturable cards remaining on the table.)

♦ An Ace (counting as one) or number card below Ten captures *one* card such that the ranks of the played and captured cards add up to 10.

♦ Because a Five naturally captures its own rank, it also must capture all three Fives if all three are on the table.

If a play results in a capture, the player gathers the played and captured cards into a scoring pile in front of them. Otherwise, the played card remains on the table to be captured by any player. Regardless of the outcome of the first card, the player then draws the top stock card and plays it, making captures in the same manner.

After the final player plays their final turn, the stock will be empty, and all cards will be captured. Each player earns points for captured cards as follows:

Card Captured	Points Awarded
Two through Eight of Hearts or Diamonds	Rank value of captured card
Nine through King of Hearts or Diamonds	10
Ace of Hearts or Diamonds	20
Ace of Spades (three or four players only)	30
Ace of Clubs (four players only)	40

In a two-player game, the player with the higher score wins. In a three-player game, any player with at least 80 points wins. In a four-player game, players must earn at least 70 points in order to win. If multiple players achieve the winning score, they are considered tied regardless of their actual scores.

Variation

Red Frog Black Frog is a Thai version with different point values awarded for captured cards:

Card Captured	Points Awarded
Two through Nine of Spades or Clubs	Rank value of captured card
Ten through King of Spades or Clubs	10
Ace of Spades	50

CONTINUED

BASRA

Reportedly played in coffee shops throughout the Middle East, Basra is particularly popular in Cyprus, Egypt, Lebanon, Greece, and Turkey.

OBJECTIVE: Have the highest score when any player or team reaches 101 points.

MATERIALS: One standard 52-card deck (no Jokers), a scorekeeping method

NUMERICAL CARD VALUES: Ace = 1, number card = rank value; face cards have no numerical value

Setup

In a four-person game, players may play in teams of two. Teammates sit opposite each other.

Dealing

Deal four cards to each player's hand. Deal the next four cards faceup in the center of the table. If any of these cards is a Jack or the Seven of Diamonds, it is shuffled back into the stock and replaced with a new card off the top. The dealer keeps the stock.

Playing the Game

In turn, a player plays one card faceup on the table. A played card will capture one or more table cards according to the following rules:

- Any played card captures cards of the same rank.

- A number card captures groups of cards whose numerical values add up to the value of the played card.

- A Jack or the Seven of Diamonds captures every card on the table.

If a play results in a capture, the player gathers the played and captured cards into a scoring pile in front of them. Otherwise, the played card remains on the table to be captured by any player.

CONTINUED

Capturing every card on the table at once is called a "basra." Each basra is worth bonus points at the end of a hand. Traditionally, a player reminds themselves of a basra by placing one of the captured cards faceup rather than facedown in their scoring pile. Capturing with a Jack does not count as a basra; however, capturing with the Seven of Diamonds counts as a basra *if* all table cards are numbered and add up to 10 or less.

Every four turns, after everyone has played their last card, the dealer gives four more cards to each player, and the hand continues. The hand is over when all players have run out of cards and there are no more cards to deal. The last player to have made a capture wins any cards remaining on the table. (This does not count as a basra.) Players earn points for their captured cards as follows:

- **30 points** for capturing the most cards in the hand (if there's a tie, these points are carried forward and awarded as a bonus to the player or team who captures the most cards in the next hand)

- **10 points** for each basra

- **3 points** for capturing the Ten of Diamonds

- **2 points** for capturing the Two of Clubs

- **1 point** for each Jack or Ace captured

Each player's or team's score for the hand is added to their total score for the game. When at least one player or team has 101 points or more, whoever has the highest score wins.

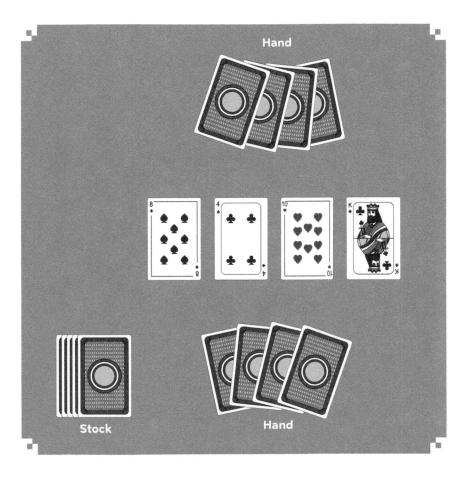

LAUGH AND LIE DOWN

This game is mentioned in European literature as early as 1522, making it one of the oldest games in this book.

OBJECTIVE: Have the most chips after five hands.

MATERIALS: One standard 52-card deck (no Jokers), betting chips

Setup

Distribute 31 betting chips to each player.

Dealing

Deal eight cards to each player's hand. Place the remaining 12 cards faceup on the table.

Immediately after the deal, if the tableau contains four of a kind, the dealer captures both pairs. If any player holds four of a kind in their hand, they capture both pairs. If they hold three of a kind, they capture *two* of the matching cards. All other pairs they hold remain in their hand for the time being.

Playing the Game

At the start of a hand, the dealer pays three chips into a central pot. The other players pay two chips each. In turn, each player plays one card from their hand to capture one or three (never two) tableau cards of the same rank as the played card. Captured pairs are placed faceup beside or in front of the player who captured them. If another player has a pair in their hand that matches the rank of a pair already captured, they may announce it and place it with their captured pairs. If a player can't make a capture on their turn (possibly because the tableau is empty), they place their entire hand faceup in the tableau and sit out the remainder of the hand. Their cards are now available to be captured.

Another way to capture cards is to spot and claim mistakes made by other players. All players, including those who have already laid down their hands, may do this. Players may claim:

- Four of a kind from the tableau, if the dealer fails to claim it.

- The remaining pair, if a player captures only one of three matching cards in the tableau.

- Pairs from a laid-down hand that the hand's owner should have already captured.

A hand ends when all but one player's hand is empty. The player with cards remaining captures all remaining tableau cards and wins five chips from the pot. Any player who captured fewer than four pairs pays one chip to the pot for each pair they fell short. Those who captured more than four pairs win one chip for each pair above four. (This should leave the pot empty.)

At the end of five hands, the player with the most chips wins.

Variations

The game can be adapted for different numbers of players by changing a few numbers, including the target capture count (the number of pairs above or below which a player wins or loses chips):

Number of Players/Hands	3	4	6
Hand Cards Dealt	13	10	7
Tableau Cards Dealt	13	12	10
Target Capture Count	7	5	3
Dealer Initial Bet	4	3	3
Nondealer Initial Bet	3	2	2
Chips Won by Last Player with Cards in Hand	5	3	5

CONTINUED

CASINO

Casino is the only fishing game to achieve significant popularity in the English-speaking world.

OBJECTIVE: Be the first player to reach 21 points.

MATERIALS: One standard 52-card deck (no Jokers), a scorekeeping method

NUMERICAL CARD VALUES: Ace = 1, number card = rank value; face cards have no numerical value

Dealing

Deal four cards to each player's hand and four more faceup on the table. The dealer keeps the stock.

Playing the Game

In turn, each player plays one card faceup to perform one of the following actions:

+ **Building:** The card may be "built" onto a tableau card or pile; the value of the resulting pile is equal to the combined values of the cards within it. A player who builds must have a card in their hand of the same value as the resulting pile. Built piles should be fanned so their contents are visible.

+ **Augmenting:** The card may be placed on a card or pile *of equal value to itself* to "augment" it. The resulting pile retains the value of the original card or pile; it can be augmented further but can no longer be built upon. A player who augments must have a card in their hand of the same value as the resulting pile.

+ **Combining:** The card may be combined with loose (non-piled) cards on the table and *then* used to build or augment. The combination is treated like a single card worth the combined values of the cards within it.

CONTINUED

- **Capturing:** The card may capture all of the following from the tableau:

  - Any card or pile of the same value as the played card

  - Any group of cards or piles whose values add up to that of the played card

  Captured cards, along with the played card, are taken into the player's scoring pile.

- **Trailing:** The card may be discarded into the tableau with no further action. It becomes available for any player to capture.

Face cards can't be built or augmented; they must be captured by cards of the same rank. If three matching face cards are present in the tableau, they are all captured together. If two are present, only one may be captured (otherwise, it becomes impossible to capture the fourth).

Every four turns, after everyone has played their last card, the dealer gives four more cards to each player, and the hand continues. The hand is over when all players' hands are empty and there are no more cards to deal. The last player to have made a capture wins any cards remaining on the table. Players earn points for cards captured during the hand as follows:

- **3 points** for the most cards

- **2 points** for the Ten of Diamonds

- **1 point** for the most Spades

- **1 point** for the Two of Spades

- **1 point** per Ace

If there's a tie in any category, nobody wins the points for that category. Each player's score for the hand is added to their total score for the game. When one or more players reach 21 points, the player with the highest score wins.

Variations

- **Royal Casino:** See page 216.

- **Sweep Points:** Award one point each time a player "sweeps" (captures all cards currently on the table).

Player 2

Player 1

Stock

ROYAL CASINO

A variant of Casino (page 213), Royal Casino is more popular outside the English-speaking world.

OBJECTIVE: Be the first player to reach 21 points.

MATERIALS: One standard 52-card deck (no Jokers), a scorekeeping method

NUMERICAL CARD VALUES: Ace = 1 or 14, King = 13, Queen = 12, Jack = 11, number card = rank value

Dealing

Deal four cards to each player's hand and four more faceup on the table. The dealer keeps the stock.

Playing the Game

This game is played almost exactly like Casino (page 213). The main difference is that face cards have numerical value and may be built, augmented, and captured like any other card. Furthermore:

♦ The rule about only capturing one or three face cards at once no longer applies.

♦ Piles may be built to a maximum value of 14.

♦ Players earn one point each time they "sweep" (capture all cards currently on the table).

♦ An Ace is worth either 1 or 14. The value of a loose Ace in the tableau is not yet determined. When built on or used to build, an Ace is worth 1. When captured, augmented or used to augment, the value is at the discretion of the current player.

When one or more players reach 21 points, the player with the highest score wins.

Player 2

Player 1

ELÉWÉNJEWÉ

This game hails from the Yorubaland region of West Africa. Its full name is Eléwénjewénómbàjenómbà.

OBJECTIVE: Capture the most cards in four hands.

MATERIALS: One standard 52-card deck (Jokers optional), a scorekeeping method

NUMERICAL CARD VALUES: Ace = 1, number card = rank value; face cards have no numerical value

Dealing

Place the King, Queen, Jack, and Nine of Diamonds faceup on the table. Deal four cards to each player's hand. The dealer keeps the stock.

Playing the Game

Each turn, a player plays one card faceup on the table. They may capture any table cards of equal rank to their played card *and* any groups of table cards whose numerical values add up to the value of their played card. They are *not* required to take all (or any) possible captures. If included, Jokers capture every card on the table. When a player captures, they place the played and captured cards into a scoring pile in front of them. If they don't capture, the played card remains on the table.

When everyone has played their last card, the dealer gives four more cards to each player, and the hand continues. The hand is over when all players' hands are empty and there are no more cards to deal. Whoever captures the most cards over the course of four hands wins.

TOTIT

Like a fine coffee, Totit (pronounced "TOHT-it") comes from the Indonesian island of Java.

OBJECTIVE: Score the most points over a set number of hands.

MATERIALS: Two standard 52-card decks (no Jokers)

Setup

Remove the following from both decks:

+ Tens and face cards of Hearts, Clubs, and Diamonds

+ All Spades *except* the face cards

Dealing

Deal 18 cards faceup on the table and seven cards to each player's hand.

Playing the Game

Each turn, a player plays one card faceup on the table. A played card will capture a table card according to the following rules:

+ On a player's first turn, a played card captures an identical card (same rank and suit).

+ On any other turn, a played card captures one card of the same rank. Aces and face cards are all treated as if they have the same rank (in other words, they can all capture each other). A captured card *can't* be identical to the played card unless there is no choice.

If a play results in a capture, the player places the played and captured cards into a scoring pile in front of them. Otherwise, the played card remains on the table. Players take turns playing cards until everyone's hand is empty.

For each pair of identical cards (same rank and suit) that they captured during the hand, a player adds one point to their total score for the game. After each player has been the dealer once, the player with the highest score wins.

SEEP

Popular throughout North India and Pakistan, Seep has similar mechanics to Casino (page 213) yet maintains a character all its own.

OBJECTIVE: Beat the other team by 100 or more points.

MATERIALS: One standard 52-card deck (no Jokers), a scorekeeping method

NUMERICAL CARD VALUES: Ace = 1, Jack = 11, Queen = 12, King = 13, number card = rank value

Setup

Players pair up in teams of two. Teammates sit opposite each other.

Dealing

Deal four cards to the starting player's hand and four cards facedown on the table. If the starting player has no cards higher than an Eight, reshuffle and redeal all cards until they do. Cards will be dealt to other players once the starting player has played a card, according to the instructions on page 224.

Game Structure

Game play centers around creating and capturing "houses," fanned piles in the tableau that can be captured as a unit. Cards not contained in a house are called "loose." Each house has a numerical value between 9 and 13 and one or more "owners." Until a house is captured (either by them or an opponent) or they are relieved of ownership, a player must *always* have a card in their hand of equal value to any house they own (or co-own). This card may be used to capture the house on their turn. There can never be more than one house of the same value at the same time.

In order to create, change, or capture houses, each player on their turn uses one card from their hand to perform one of the following actions:

- **Build a House:** The card may be combined with one or more loose tableau cards to create a house, which is owned by the player who created it. The value is the sum of the values of the cards within it (minimum 9, maximum 13) and must match a card of the same value (9 through 13) in the player's hand.

- **Break a House:** The card may be added to a house *belonging to another player* (opponent or teammate) to "break" it. The house has a new value, equal to its starting value plus the value of the added card, and the breaker becomes its owner.

- **Cement a House:** A "cemented" house is made up of two or more units of numerical value (houses, loose cards, or groups of loose cards) that are equal to one another. Cemented houses are created in two ways:

  - Combining the played card with a house, loose card, or group of loose cards that's of equal value to itself.

  - Performing a build or break action that *creates* a house that's equal in value to a house, loose card, or group of loose cards in the tableau.

  The matching units of value are combined together in one fanned pile. A cemented house has the same value that each unit had before being combined. Cemented houses can be cemented again but can't be broken. If a player cements a house that's owned by an opponent, they become a co-owner. If they cement a house owned by their teammate, the teammate retains sole ownership.

- **Capture:** When not played to build, break, or cement a house, a card captures *every* house, loose card, and group of loose cards in the tableau that is of equal value to the played card. The played card and captured cards are taken into the player's scoring pile.

- **Trail:** If no other actions are available, a card may be discarded into the tableau with no further action. It becomes available for any player to capture.

Capturing every card currently on the table is called a "sweep" (or "seep") and is worth bonus points. Traditionally, a player reminds themselves of the sweep by placing one of the captured cards faceup rather than facedown in their scoring pile.

CONTINUED

Playing the Game

The starting player begins by "bidding for a house," declaring a value between 9 and 13 that matches the numerical value of a card in their hand. The dealer then turns up the four tableau cards. As their first turn, the bidder must either build a house worth the same value as the bid, capture a card of the same value as the bid, or trail a card worth the same value as the bid.

Once the bidder has played, the dealer continues dealing, starting with the player *after* the bidder and giving four cards at a time to each player until everyone has 12 (except the starting player, who has already played one). Beginning with the dealer's partner, players take turns playing one card faceup and performing one of the actions described on page 223.

When all players have run out of cards, the last player to have made a capture wins any loose cards remaining on the table (there should be no houses remaining). Points for captured cards (including those contained within houses) are awarded as follows:

+ **Points equal to the card's numerical value** for each Spade captured

+ **1 point** for each Ace captured (don't double-count the Ace of Spades)

+ **6 points** for capturing the Ten of Diamonds

+ **50 points** per sweep, with two exceptions:

  + A sweep on the *first* turn of the hand is worth 25 points

  + A sweep on the *last* turn of the hand is worth no points

Each team's score for the hand is added to their total score for the game. The first team to have at least 100 points more than their opponents wins.

SCOPA

LENGTH OF PLAY: 10 TO 15 MINUTES PER HAND

One of the biggest card games in Italy, this game has a name that literally means "broom."

OBJECTIVE: Have the highest score when any player or team reaches 11 points or more.

MATERIALS: One standard 52-card deck (no Jokers), a scorekeeping method

NUMERICAL CARD VALUES: Ace = 1, Jack = 8, Queen = 9, King = 10, number card = rank value

Setup

Twelve cards must be removed from the deck. There are two ways of doing this:

+ **Numerical Deck:** Remove the Jacks, Queens, and Kings. (Easier for beginners.)
+ **Milanese Deck:** Remove the Eights, Nines, and Tens. (More traditional.)

Dealing

Deal three cards to each player's hand. Deal the next four cards faceup in the center of the table. If more than two of these cards are Tens or Kings, gather all four back into the stock, shuffle, and redeal the table layout. The dealer keeps the stock.

Playing the Game

On their turn, each player plays one card faceup on the table. A played card will capture one table card of the same rank. If a card of the same rank is not available, the card will capture one group of table cards whose numerical values add up to the value of the played card. Players are not required to play a card that makes a capture; however, if the card played can make a capture, the capture is not optional.

If a play results in a capture, the player gathers the played and captured cards into a scoring pile in front of them. Otherwise, the played card remains on the table to be captured by any player.

Capturing every card on the table at once is called a "scopa." Each scopa is worth one bonus point at the end of a hand. Traditionally, a player reminds themselves of a scopa by placing one of the captured cards faceup rather than facedown in their scoring pile.

Every three turns, after everyone has played their last card, the dealer gives three more cards to each player, and the hand continues. The hand is over when all players have run out of cards and there are no more cards to deal. The last player to have made a capture wins any cards remaining on the table. (This does not count as a scopa.) Players earn points for their captured cards as follows:

+ **1 point** for each scopa

+ **1 point** for capturing the most cards in the hand (if there's a tie, no one wins the point)

+ **1 point** for capturing the most Diamond cards (if there's a tie, no one wins the point)

+ **1 point** for capturing the Seven of Diamonds

One final point is awarded for the highest value Primiera. A Primiera is a group of four cards, one of each suit, formed from a player's or team's captured cards. If a player or team doesn't have at least one card of each suit, they can't make a Primiera. Each rank of card has a Primiera value that is separate from its normal numerical value (see the table below). The value of the Primiera is the sum of the Primiera values of the cards it contains. If there's a tie for highest Primiera, nobody wins the Primiera point.

Card Rank	Seven	Six	Ace	Five	Four	Three	Two	Eight, Nine, Ten, Jack, Queen, or King
Primiera Value	21	18	16	15	14	13	12	10

Each player or team's score for the hand is added to their total score for the game. When at least one player or team has 11 points or more, whoever has the highest score wins.

CONTINUED

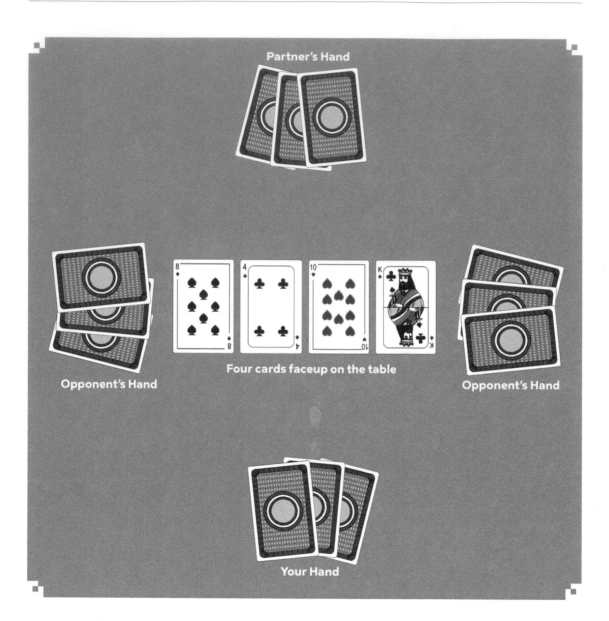

Partner's Hand

Opponent's Hand

Four cards faceup on the table

Opponent's Hand

Your Hand

INDEX OF CARD GAMES

INDEX BY NUMBER OF PLAYERS

ACKNOWLEDGMENTS

Extreme thanks to my wife, the love of my life, who endures my creative insanity and still supports me.

My daughters, thanks for your patience during the writing process—and for making me take breaks to have fun!

DJ and DJ, *gomawo* for teaching me Canasta and Cribbage. Do you believe it's not a scam yet?

Ash Ryan

Thank you, family and friends, for your patience and love—especially during card games! (I told you I'd eventually write the book on this.)

C. S. Kaiser

From both of us, thanks to SK for the research help, encouragement, and awesome spreadsheet!

The Triple S Legion, without whom our content would go unnoticed. :SincerityHands:

And our editor Van, plus the rest of the team at Rockridge Press!

ABOUT THE AUTHORS

 **Ash Ryan** is a lifelong cardplayer and all-around gamer. He's also a writer, podcast host, and video producer. In 2011, he left his corporate media-production job to raise his two daughters and write a sci-fi adventure novel. He's now writing a better sci-fi adventure novel.

 **C. S. Kaiser** is a skilled player and manipulator of cards in addition to being a writer and game development consultant. After spending most of his life struggling to communicate, he now makes a career of speaking and writing for video games, podcasts, and his own expansive fantasy book series.

Both authors enjoy small-town life in the glorious (and often snow-covered) Canadian prairies. In 2015, they founded the Triple S League, a YouTube channel dedicated to video game guides and lore.

9 781638 786528